# HOW AND WHY GOD EVOLVED

## AN ALTERNATIVE PERSPECTIVE

BABAR SHAH KHAN

# HOW AND WHY GOD EVOLVED
# AN ALTERNATIVE PERSPECTIVE

*iUniverse books may be ordered through booksellers or by contacting:*

*iUniverse*
*1663 Liberty Drive*
*Bloomington, IN 47403*
*www.iuniverse.com*
*1-800-Authors (1-800-288-4677)*

*Abdullah Yusuf Ali, trans., The Qur'an, S ed. (Tahrike Tarsile Qur'an Inc., 2005). All references to the Qur'an are from this edition and are noted by surah and verse.*

*The NRSV Notetaker's Bible: New Revised Standard Version with the Apocrypha (Oxford University Press, 2009). All references to the Bible are from this edition.*

*ISBN: 978-1-4917-6881-5 (sc)*
*ISBN: 978-1-4917-6883-9 (hc)*
*ISBN: 978-1-4917-6882-2 (e)*

*Library of Congress Control Number: 2015909591*

*Print information available on the last page.*

*iUniverse rev. date: 8/11/2015*

To my father, Akbar Shah Khan, whose love for writing inspired me to believe that I was capable of authoring a book. He wrote a book in the early 1930s and continued writing until his last days. He defied many traditional, cultural, social, and religious doctrines of the time; stood up against considerable odds; and guided us kids with reason and logic.

To my loving wife, Monika, who sat with me—sometimes sleepily, and other times wide awake—listening attentively through my many ramblings about God, no God, and the universe. She always gave me her full and cheerful support.

# CONTENTS

# INTRODUCTION

Here are just a few thoughts to consider before you read this book. Please keep in mind my intents: to highlight certain facts about holy verses and to clarify some misguided interpretations of these verses. However knowledgeable, apostles, preachers, and scholars inevitably bring their own experiences and beliefs to any religious text, and these conscious and subconscious beliefs can cause writers and readers to put a spin on the scriptures. In pointing out misinterpretations of holy scriptures and exploring some of the political reasons involved, the author does not intend to deride believers of any religion. The author also intends to show how human notions of God throughout history have created some bizarre and even dangerous social conditions.

This book highlights the link among pagan, polytheistic, and monotheistic beliefs. In human history, first there were many gods, followed by one God, followed by the three-in-one God. Did you know that humans, not God, came up with the concept of the Trinity? With the addition of the Trinity, Christianity became something of a strange contraption, sort of like a Rolls-Royce with square wheels and no steering wheel. God's character, then, changed according to humanity's changes. This fact is a strong indicator that humans helped create God in stages, and designed Him to serve a variety of purposes—each group according to its cultural norms and sociopolitical agenda. It's as if the writers of holy books fine-tuned ancient Egyptian and Greek myths and legends into their own divine recipe books; with their own respective spices, they reseasoned earlier scriptures, and each claimed to have invented a brand-new book, a revolutionary cookbook. Earlier, visible stone gods had a tough time answering questions, solving problems, and maintaining order in the universe. Creating a new, invisible God was a wise choice on the part of Abraham! Moving God to an invisible realm shielded Him from prying hands and eyes and made the lives of Moses, Jesus, and Muhammad much easier. There are no grounds upon which to prove God wrong, just as Abraham, Moses, Jesus, and Muhammad had no grounds upon which to prove themselves right. Even God's witnesses (angels) live invisibly in an invisible realm. The whole idea of invisible entities ruins the possibility that God will prove His existence in a way that humans can detect. It is ironic that all invisible entities are made for living, visible human beings! What good are these invisible witnesses for the invisible God, who rules from an invisible throne in seventh heaven, if the jury cannot see or hear them? So how do we get to know where God is? This book answers these and many other questions for the curious reader.

# 1

## EARLY CIVILIZATIONS CREATED GOD AND GODS

To arrive at your own beliefs about God, you must first explore the history of how humanity came to form a concept of God. Equally important is understanding how other religions conceive of God. Thinking that you can understand God by yourself, as if in a vacuum, is one of the more bizarre ideas found among believing people. Believers of every religion repeat the mantra "My God," but what does the average believer know about God? What do any of us know? The notion of God, gods, and divine power took many twists and turns before settling into today's well-known categories of polytheism and monotheism. Furthermore, each of those categories has its own complexities. Among the monotheistic faiths, for example, critical differences exist between the God of Moses and the Christian, Trinitarian God. Put simplistically, the God of the Old Testament seems bent on fixing rules and laying down the law, with all its attendant punishments, while the New Testament shows God as more benevolent, more interested in engaging human beings in a loving relationship. The ensuing notion of the Holy Trinity became one of the most divisive beliefs in religious history—and like the Trinity, the very concept of divinity, or God itself, can be seen as a human invention designed to serve a variety of human purposes.

Indeed, humans make and break religious notions and rules frequently, usually to fulfill their own interests. We have only to look at the story of King Henry VIII to see this principle in action. Religious calendars, created thousands of years ago, represent a drop in the ocean of all existence on earth, yet humans see the world largely according to their ancient religious beliefs. They continue to use and abuse religious ideas for the sake of conquest or political gain, or even just to bolster their will to survive. So what "good" is religion, anyway? What does it mean to say you believe in God, and how do you evaluate this belief? Do people take on religious ideas blindly (and if so, with what consequences) or through a process of critical thinking? This book will look at these questions in further depth.

Humans come from a long tradition of hunting and killing to survive. When the first humans needed a meal, they did not hesitate to kill Bambi passing nearby. But today, if a fast and furious cheetah attacks another creature to meet its needs, we label it a "wild beast." Humans took control of animals and proclaimed themselves superior to them. We began to trade and sell animals and subdue them to fulfill certain exclusive roles, such as food, transportation, and hunting companion. Next, we began to assert "superiority" over fellow humans, forcing our rules upon the weak, the stubborn, or the just plain different. In early human existence, the stronger humans survived and set rules for the others. This plan of action didn't always work, however; a strong body can subdue a weaker body, but not necessarily a weaker body with a strong mind.

This is where religion (or God) makes an appearance as a solution to this dilemma about power. As the seventeenth-century French philosopher Voltaire said, "If God did not exist, it would be necessary to invent him."[1] Humankind needed a supreme or super power, and depending on their region or culture, humans called this power by many names, such as Ra, God, Yahweh, Lord, and Allah. Some humans even called themselves messengers of God or claimed to be divine in their own right. As time passed, language slowly changed to incorporate religion into the human psyche. Words like *heaven* and *hell*, and *soul* and *spirit*, began to appear—all adding a new level of meaning to human life and fostering hopes for a better life after death. People began to behave according to the various codes of conduct bestowed upon humanity by

---

[1] "Voltaire," *WikiQuotes*, http://en.wikiquote.org/wiki/Voltaire (2 October 2014).

these gods or God. Eventually, humanity acquired the ability to describe the nature or character of God.

According to the vast majority of monotheistic believers, God is strictly male in nature. We rarely hear God referred to as "She," despite the previous existence of matriarchal religions. Male-oriented for thousands of years now, Western society must view God as male to preserve supreme power in male hands. Simply by calling God "He," we participate in this social power play, ensuring that men retain their authoritative position. God is not only male but also omnipresent, omniscient, and omnipotent. There is no escaping God as a male source of power. Many believers of monotheist faiths accept these qualities of God, no questions asked. People continue to hold a strong and firm belief in these qualities as core components of the nature of God.

For such a strong, authoritative supreme power, God seems to *need* Abraham, Noah, Jesus, and Muhammad more than they need Him— an observation that dispels the idea of omnipotence. God created a huge flood, for example, but couldn't do much without Noah, the ark's architect and captain. God had to use Abraham to establish His contract with humanity and spread His Word. God couldn't do without Moses either; He gave Moses the Ten Commandments, a central component of Judaism, to enlighten the rest of the world. God also needed Jesus to suffer the death penalty and then disappear in order to reappear, allowing for the rise of Christianity. Another triumphant religious story, the story of Islam, is incomplete without a man named Muhammad. It seems God can't survive on His own. Without Abraham, Moses, Jesus, and Muhammad, the three major monotheistic religions are like a human body without a soul.

God also needed highly imaginative figures like Gabriel and other angels to serve as messengers between Himself and humans. But if God holds vast knowledge, power, and presence everywhere, why would He need help from puny humans and lesser angelic beings? This could suggest that humans created the character of God, with all the human talents and flaws, but on a grander scale. After all, the writers of the Old Testament gave God the character of a human ruler at their particular time in history—at once patient, generous, merciful, and forgiving, yet wrathful, harsh, and cruel. In the Bible's Exodus 20:5, God shows His more irascible side; failing to obey His orders brings about dreadful punishments. "For, I, the Lord your God am a jealous God," He says, and He punishes children "for the iniquity of parents, to the third and fourth generation of those who reject me."[2] As God Himself admits, He is jealous in nature—another quality that denotes human weakness due to insecurity. In the Old Testament, God appears as an insecure old tyrant. Today's Old Testament scholars can't rewrite Exodus 20:5, so instead they try to redefine this jealousy, distinguishing between the rightful jealousy of God and the weak-minded jealousy of humans.

Abraham, Moses, Jesus, and Muhammad reduced the multiple gods of polytheism to one God. Followers of Jesus, however, although claiming to embrace monotheism, created another unique concept of God, making Jesus part of God by referring to Him as the "Son of God." So in human history, first there were many ancient gods, followed by one God, followed by the Father/Son God, followed by the three-in-one God (Trinity). If this was all the work of human brainpower, it was influenced by a few geniuses able to mesmerize billions of followers. We see such followers today, in Mecca, eyes open in a kind of trance, walking blindly around a piece of stone that supposedly came from heaven. Muhammad and his companions didn't know that trillions of asteroids had been floating around in space for billions of years (and will continue to float for billions of years more). The notion of a holy space stone landing in Mecca calls to mind a certain belief from early human history that asserted that deities exist in stones, and that when one falls from the sky (i.e., heaven, or the place of the gods), it is a "holy" event.[3] It seems ironic that Islam, which condemns idol worship, takes an almost worshipful view of the stone in Mecca. But what makes this stone holy? Human belief itself might be the

---

[2] *The NRSV Notetaker's Bible* (Oxford University Press, 2009).

[3] "Theistic and Animistic Beliefs of the Supernatural: High Gods, Supreme Being, Spirits and Ancestor Worship," Academica.edu, last modified October 8, 2014, http://www.academia.edu/3126528/ Theistic_and_Animistic_Beliefs_of_the_Supernatural_ High_Gods_Supreme_Being_Spirits_and_Ancestor_Worship.

answer. Once humans have accepted a belief, it doesn't matter to them how contrary it is to science.

Another example of religious irony is the importance of the moon in Islam. Ages ago, the Sumerian culture of South Mesopotamia worshipped a moon deity. Pagans directly venerated the moon in each of its three phases. They associated the new moon with virginity, the full moon with motherhood, and the dark moon with fate. The moon is still a significant symbol in Middle Eastern cultures after more than five thousand years. The flags of many Muslim countries bear the symbol of the moon and stars. The moon also features prominently in certain aspects of Islam. The biggest Muslim celebration, the Eid festival, does not begin until religious officials see the new moon; the same tenet holds true for the important religious event of Ramadan. We have to wonder if, for Muslims, the moon holds a mystical connection with God. Given the strict Islamic edict against idol worship or anything that even appears to set up partners with God, such a connection would seem unlikely. And yet many orthodox Muslims who glimpse the new moon raise their hands in prayer, which can take on the dangerous appearance of moon worshipping. For some Muslims, there's a very fine line between sighting the moon and praising Allah.

Deities, prophets, and preachers have strongly guarded, controlled, and promoted the idea of religion based solely on blind faith and trust. Reason and evidence typically haven't played a part in religious ideas, although people have tried. This could be why so many deities—God, El, Yahweh, Lord, Krishna, and a hundred others—popped up at certain times: the gods served to satisfy human wishes at different times for different reasons. This could also explain why all deities were about as intelligent as the people who created them. At the beginning of human history, people put their trust and faith in stones, trees, and the sun as gods. Belief based on physical objects worked well at that time. Eventually, as people began to worship objects, the concept of religion was born. Evidence or proof of God has always been difficult to establish, despite the efforts of holy messengers. God kept sending holy books, and messengers confirmed, challenged, or created the moral codes of the day.

As we will see, God picked messengers, who picked disciples, who picked local preachers and priests to spread His Word.

Disciples and messengers also served the purpose of promoting the authenticity of their holy messenger. Before Jesus, John the Baptist appeared, and after Muhammad came Abu Bakr. Later, four supporters of Jesus known as Matthew, Mark, Luke, and John (that is, writers using their names), compiled four books called the Gospels. These stories, which sound like an eyewitness described events in vivid detail, passed by word of mouth through generations. Preachers and believers quote their holy books with unshakeable faith. Their firm beliefs and stories about God, heaven and hell, Judgment Day, Satan, the birth of Jesus, and many other events and figures, stand like a rock. There are no grounds to prove them wrong, as holy messengers had no grounds to prove themselves right. It's equivalent to some Muslims' claim that God lives in "seventh heaven." Can anyone argue that God dwells instead in first or second heaven?

Prominent writers, researchers, professors, and news media personnel all work carefully to verify their sources and stories. Today, in broadcast journalism, people try their best to confirm any story before it goes on the air. At times, however, they are proven wrong; these errors may be intentional (perhaps for political purposes) or unintentional. In ancient times, God's voice came through holy messengers. Abraham, Moses, Jesus, and Muhammad went to mind-boggling lengths (sometimes even to heaven!) in search of God and to promote God's messages, but they failed to explore the remote boundaries of earth called the Americas or Australia.

At one time, geographers thought the southwestern-most point of Portugal, called Sagres, was the western edge of earth, until the age of exploration—the fifteenth to seventeenth centuries—changed the world map. In Europe, the Portuguese introduced exploration, followed by the Italians, Spanish, English, and Dutch. As humans became more civilized, their awareness of the world grew. Likewise, humankind's sense of God developed in proportion to its own progress. In Noah's time, people had a rudimentary concept of God. He appeared as a sensitive character who engaged easily with humans; He thought, acted, and behaved like humans of His day. In the Bible's Genesis 11:7, God uses colloquial language, like "Come, let's go down and confuse their language there, so they will not understand each other's speech." Common phrases like "let's go down" fit the speech of a human leader, not the remote and regal Almighty God. Anyway, why did God need to confuse the humans who tried to build the Tower of Babel? What was He trying to do? His juvenile desire to confuse others suggests that the early God had poor judgment and an immature ego, mirroring humanity at that stage of development.

The fact that God's character changes according to humanity's changes is a strong indicator that humanity helps "create" God or the notion of God. God can progress only as far as humankind's ability to conceive of and describe Him. As the human brain developed and achieved once unimaginable goals, so did God's strength and knowledge. Humans gifted the Lord with attributes like omnipotence, omniscience, and omnipresence. This new God had all the power He needed to deal with, and even subdue, the masses.

Here is a good example of how the human brain, and therefore God, evolved. Forget about the Tower of Babel's height, a mere three hundred feet. Thousands of years later, humans started building skyscrapers all over the earth, intruding into the vicinity of seventh heaven. But at the brink of modern times, God did not say, "Let's go down to confuse them." Apparently He learned from humans another talent: diplomacy. Despite being omnipotent, omniscient, and omnipresent, God couldn't go it alone; He was still in desperate need of human help. Every time He needed help relaying a message, He called upon his favorites, holy messengers, judges, and kings—three ideal characters at work in the human mind. Without holy messengers, God is a lame duck, pushed along by the current with no direction.

In the history of humankind, from the first divine messenger to the last (124,000 in total, according to the Bible), human life improved at a snail's pace. Life from birth to death involved great hardship, physical and emotional. It's no wonder, then, that people began to seek out words of hope for a better life after death. Humans had to have something to look forward to and some reason to mind their manners if they were going to put up with life as it was. Their concepts of God, the Messiah, heaven, hell, and religion helped promote some semblance of an orderly life here on earth in exchange for a rosy existence after death.

Humankind's general condition has improved enormously in the last two hundred years, following the Industrial Revolution. More of us today have the basic needs of life met, such as food, shelter, and medical care. Our comfortable homes protect us from frigid or scorching temperatures. Instead of using camel carts, we travel more quickly in luxury cars with climate control. God's first spoken words in the Old Testament, Genesis 1:3, are "Let there be light." In the time it took God to say this, maybe two seconds, He created light. Today, human beings flip a switch in fewer than two seconds and light appears. All this has happened, of course, without any guidance from popes, priests, and heavenly messengers.

Despite today's comforts, some people continue to yearn for earlier times. One phrase people can't seem to rid themselves of is "the good old days." My sincere suggestion to such people is to take their pick of the good old days of Moses, Jesus, or Muhammad, and go back in time for seven days at their own risk. Why not try it here, going back to the time of Moses. (The Qur'an mentions him more times than it does Muhammad, so Moses clearly stands out from the rest of the 123,999 messengers.) Before you go on this seven-day tour, however, here are a few important tips to keep in mind:

1. Whether you're right or wrong, don't get into a fight in front of mighty Moses. He has a bad habit of solving other people's problems uninvited, using his fist rather than his brain. Remember: you'll survive in the presence of Moses only if you are an Israelite, anyway.
2. Don't count exclusively on Moses's help, as he sometimes disappears for a long time.
3. Don't sign up for any journeys with Moses; it will take forty years, and you'll go in circles.
4. Ask Moses if you can carry the Ten Commandments back from Mount Sinai, and be sure to place them in bubble wrap (because you know he dropped them once before).

5.  Watch out for the ten plagues of Egypt. No medical aid will be available.
6.  If you are an Egyptian or an Israelite, don't mention it; either God or Pharaoh will get you.

Whenever we speak of how humans conceive of God, we have to address the beginning of Satan, who appears in all holy books and stands as the counterbalancing force to the character of God. Satan's goal was to derail human beings from the godly path and mislead them to evil. God, in turn, created heaven and hell to reward or punish humans according to how well they stay on the godly path. If there were no penalty or punishment, people would run free, like loose cannons. Thanks to Satan, however, they have a reason to fear the torments of hell and behave themselves. Satan also serves the purpose of making God's character appear perfect, pure, and flawless. (If only Adam had ignored the ill-advised guidance of Satan, then he and all of humanity would be enjoying life in the Garden of Eden, wrapped in fig leaves, as pure and flawless as God Himself). For God to be God, He has to be perfect. Humanity wants God to be flawless, a perfect 10. What would happen, however, if God registered only a 9.9876543210 on the perfect 10 scale? Would we think of the world as less perfect and more chaotic and anarchic? The earth would continue on as it always has: rotating on its axis, causing all the seasons with their ensuing beauties and natural disasters.

Because humans want a perfect God, God naturally has to have authority over everyone. In human hands, He controlled His kingdom by inciting fear and threatening His wrath and punishment, as the Old Testament reveals. But if God was a tyrant to be feared, He was also, oddly enough, the only source of goodness and the only hope for forgiveness. Early pupils of God's messengers, religious pundits, and defenders of faith held out the greatest hope of all: that God has a soft and forgiving side too. Of course, that hasn't stopped wrongdoers from committing grave crimes and then simply saying, "God understands, and He will forgive us." It remains a mystery, though, how and why people came to this self-confirmed belief that "God will forgive us," as if they could understand His mind. Defenders of all faiths so often believe this about God, despite never having seen or heard Him. They deliver this statement of belief with an authority that suggests they are His business or social partners for eternity.

Christians went a step further and made Jesus a vehicle for the forgiveness of sins. In doing so, however, they changed the nature of God. Jesus as part God threw a spanner into the divine wheel, and some explanation had to be made for this. Christians then came up with the notion of the Trinity as a handy, albeit confusing, solution. According to the doctrine of the Trinity, God is three in one: Father, Son, and Holy Ghost. God came to earth from heaven as Jesus, died on a cross to give His life for human sins, and later, presumably also whirled around in the sky as a ghost. So what happens to the unlucky millions of human beings who lived before Jesus came to earth—the ones who never heard His teachings? Yet again, the Christians have an answer: John 1:1 states that in the beginning was the Word and the Word was with God, and the Word was God. Next, "the Word became 'flesh' and lived among us, and we have seen his glory, the glory as of a father's only son full, of grace and truth" (John 1:14). The Word turned into the physical body of Jesus Christ. It's a bit of a hodgepodge theory, created by defenders of faith, to assert that their particular messiah, Jesus, and their particular religion, Christianity, is truly original and better than the rest.

The Trinity (or "God in Three Persons" or the "Triune" God) works as follows: God the Father = Jesus the Son (The Word Made Flesh) = the Holy Ghost. God the Father sent God the Son (Jesus), and the Holy Spirit followed. They are separate components of one overarching God. Not even God's holy messengers or the Messiah Himself have been able to explain any of this. Although Christians tried their best, there exists no right answer that the average human brain can comprehend. It's as if a mathematics student were to prove that two plus two equals four by first multiplying the square root of 12345, subtracting half the square root of .012345, adding the log of 98765, and dividing that by all the odd numbers: 1, 3, 5, 7, and 9. Someone completely new to mathematics, of course, might be astounded by the awesome, complex mysteries of this math.

Worshippers all over the world gather regularly on Fridays, Saturdays, or Sundays—or even daily, depending on their particular faiths. The holy pope, as well as your average priest, preacher, rabbi, or mullah gives his divine musings to the devoted day in and day out. Humble listeners, like our neophyte mathematics student, keep coming back without asking hard questions or challenging the authority of God or His representatives. Have you ever seen someone raise his or her hand to challenge the authority of God or a prayer leader in a church, mosque, synagogue, or temple? Now think for a minute about the fate of a challenger who would raise his hand in the midst of fellow worshippers. He might be harassed verbally—or perhaps even physically harmed—and dared to come back. Ironically, the modest flock of God that had assembled peacefully just minutes earlier would be ready to beat the daylights out of this innocent, if curious, challenger.

Let me draw a parallel between the status of teachers and the human-conceived character of God. Teachers once symbolized knowledge, which we know equals power. At one time, students quietly listened to their teachers, respected them, and posed no challenges to them. Students were tried, tested, and scored, but teachers were not. This dynamic sounds similar to the authority God has over His subjects. In biblical times, no one dared challenge the authority and power of God. Humans craftily created God's character to make Him capable of delivering a whole regimen of punishments, even the threat of hell, for the sin of disobedience. Therefore, the majority of people were strongly inclined toward belief in God (rather than no belief). Those who weren't so sure often chose to believe anyway—to be on the safe side, so to speak, in hopes of security a seat in heaven on Judgment Day. This way, believers would lose nothing, even if it turned out that God did not exist. Some believers say that they receive blessings from God and that God answers their prayers. They offer sacrifices of goats, lambs, or cows, or they pray profusely, offering more than the required number of prayers, expecting God to help them solve their earthly problems in return. In a sense, they are bartering with God: "I believe in You. Now help me out." But the fact remains: no atheist god waits to punish believers for their faith. Believers, nonbelievers, agnostics, and atheists ride together in same boat here in this world.

Believers persist in thinking that God will come to their aid, saying,

"God helps those who help themselves." That phrase, which highlights the importance of taking initiative in overcoming one's daily troubles, is overused by people of all faiths and regularly mistaken as scripture. In fact, according to a survey, 81 percent of believers are under the impression that this quotation originated in the Bible.[4] It does not; nevertheless, it often tops the list of most widely known Bible verses. Only the Qur'an comes close to containing this phrase, in Surah 22:40: "God will aid those who aid His cause."[5] There is nothing noble about this aid from God, who expects something in return. It sounds a lot like the common saying "You scratch my back and I'll scratch yours." It seems that prayers are about as useful as these common clichés. Unanswered most of the time, prayers are like the throw of the dice on a craps table in Vegas.

Another frustrating fact for believers is that God has never shown Himself visibly in any form, even when needed the most. Moses came closest to seeing God—or, more accurately, God's back—on Mount Sinai, but shortly after that, he became unconscious and had no recollection of what he saw. Some believers say that God's presence is within us from the beginning. So why doesn't God show Himself in front of masses of people? That way, there'd be no more guessing and no more arguments. Why pick a holy messenger to spread your message when you can do it yourself? According to the Bible, the Lord told Moses, "I will come to you in a dense cloud and let the people hear Me speak to you." When God does come to town, the mountains shake, the sky thunders, and the whole place erupts with lightning bolts, smoke, and fire. But why does God choose this scenario? He could have picked a calm, beautiful day with a lovely breeze flowing through the valley of Mount Sinai. Instead, He sets up a tumultuous, mysterious scene that makes Him seem more like a magician on stage, accompanied by the usual distractions—lots of visuals and noise, and always a handy helper. Moses goes down and warns the people not to cross the boundary lines set at the foot of the

[4] "God Helps Those Who Help Themselves: Prevalence and Assessment," *Wikipedia*, last modified October 4, 2014, http://en.wikipedia.org/wiki/God_helps_those_who_help_themselves.
[5] Abdullah Yusuf Ali, trans., *The Holy Qur'an*, S ed. (Tahrike Tarsile Qur'an Inc., 2005). All references to the Qur'an are from this edition and are noted by surah and verse.

mountain, for if they do, God will rush like a flood at them. One has to wonder if Moses himself used the stormy night to set the stage for his miraculous encounter with God.

In the Gospels, however, when God should act like a magician and save Jesus from the cross, He does nothing. There is Jesus, in front of thousands of people, praying that God will come to His rescue. Such a rescue would have removed all doubt about God's existence. It could have solved a lot of problems, and even brought about world peace! The enemies of Jesus who put Him on the cross would have turned into instant believers and begged God for mercy. Everyone would have gotten Jesus's message, no questions asked. How might that rescue have changed the world? Certainly, God would not have needed to pick another prophet, Muhammad, to spread the same message again some six hundred years later.

Amazingly, God picked messengers for thousands of years with little luck. This proves that the message and the messengers were questionable at best. Those holy messengers often seemed less interested in sharing God's message than in pushing their own agendas in the pursuit of power. Self-proclaimed messiahs exist even today, trying to pass off their words as divine messages, but only the most limited numbers of human beings take them seriously. The same would be true for Moses, Jesus, and Muhammad if they were out and about preaching today. All three would have a tough time convincing the world of the veracity of their message.

It would be useful here to stop and consider how humanity got to this point of such delusion in its concepts of God and religion. The roots of human history reveal how humans created their notion of God. About seven or eight thousand years ago, the earliest known settlers, after a brief period of agricultural growth, became understandably appreciative of the sun. Not only was it the most visible object in the sky, but people recognized the link between the sun and plant growth. They came to see the sun as the giver of life. Their respect for the sun turned into reverence and then into worship. They exalted the sun as a god and gave it a name, Ra. Shortly thereafter, they began to do the same with other celestial objects—like the moon, stars, and planets—naming them and giving them godly status. Long before Abraham believed in one God, humans bowed to many gods.

The notion and images of the divine also appeared in the Norse pagan world. The Norse believed that the gods were positioned on life's many crossroads for different reasons, and they ascribed to each god a certain power, such as fertility or abundance. They also made figurines to represent the gods and showcase their individual powers. While the Norse gods had different names than other early gods, the essential concept of the divine was the same. Early Norse gods manifested humility and gentleness. Their mild-mannered nature must have had a trickle-down effect on Abraham's God, who at one point refers to Abraham as His friend. Genesis 18:1 shows God visiting Abraham in Mamre, where Abraham stayed in his tent by the oak tree in the heat of the day. Abraham's God differed greatly from the God of Moses, who appeared in boisterous fashion on Mount Sinai.

As human beings created their various images of God or gods, they took some different and some similar paths, but they always influenced one another. The early civilizations of Babylon, Mesopotamia, Assyria, and Egypt began to form distinctive local beliefs that eventually spread among them and then on to other regions. And the notion of "what works for me must work for others" is still very much alive today. For example, the idea of "democracy" is close to the hearts and minds of the Western world, despite its glaring inadequacies in reality. In recent history, America's churchgoing president George W. Bush felt a need to spread the gospel of democracy in the Middle East. He did so without considering the customs, culture, and traditions of the people there, at a cost of more than $3 trillion, 4,486 military lives, and 162,000 innocent civilian lives. On the other hand, Middle Eastern religious leaders and their brainwashed young followers, obsessed with taking Sharia law to the extreme, are hell-bent on forcing their religion on the rest of the world. But the facts show that their twisted version of Islamic law has not worked in Muslim countries for the last fourteen hundred years.

Genesis 1:26 tells us that God said, "Let us make humankind in Our image, according to Our likeness." Because God appears full of strengths and weaknesses, humankind reflects this duality of nature.

Referring to God's weaknesses, however, is generally taboo in the eyes of believers, despite the hot temper many believers ascribe to Him. The Old Testament shows God sending down blazing fires that kill innocent people. He also causes extreme heat waves in some areas that result in severe famine and drought. Heavy rainfall and flooding in other areas create a high level of danger to humans. This leaves us to wonder if some people truly believe that God intentionally created these disasters to destroy innocent people. Yet people continue to say, "God makes no mistakes," despite many periodic natural disasters.

Greek society also created gods in its own image, full of strengths and weaknesses like human beings, but on a more reasonable scale. They employed more logic in the creation of their gods than the monotheists did. Greek gods seemed to strike a balance between the gentle Norse pagan gods and the "fire and brimstone" God of the Old Testament. Greek gods were not quite as hell-bent on handing out sweepingly cruel punishments as old Yahweh was. In Greek mythology, only three people were found guilty of crimes against gods. These crimes were a great source of frustration to the gods, who meted out punishment only to the offending individuals, and in direct proportion to their offenses.

Tityos[6] admittedly met a gruesome end, having his liver plucked and eaten by vultures. Sisyphus[7] was doomed to spend eternity rolling a ball to the top of a hill, only to have it slip from his hand and come rolling back down. Tantalus[8] was left forever hungry and thirsty near a fruit-laden tree that shrank from him every time he tried to reach it, and by a pool whose water always lowered itself beyond his reach. Wrongdoers in Greek mythology served as examples of what happens when you harbor certain obsessions or other "fatal flaws." The Greek gods themselves represented various parts of the human psyche.

Monotheism was the next religion to appear, with its central character

---

[6] Aaron J. Atsma, "Tityos, Giant of the Land," Theoi.com, http://www.theoi.com/Gigante/GiganteTityos.html.

[7] "Sisyphus," *Wikipedia*, last modified October 6, 2014, http://en.wikipedia.org/wiki/Sisyphus.

[8] "Tantalus," *Wikipedia*, last modified September 1, 2013, http://en.wikipedia.org/wiki/Tantalus.

the One Supreme God, as touted by self-proclaimed holy messengers. This new and improved God came to the stage fully appareled to play the part of the All-Powerful, Ever-Present, and All-Knowing. His new costume, however, was invisible, unlike the clothing of earlier gods. His three new qualities went hand in hand with invisibility, and they made His job a lot easier. Earlier, visible gods had a tough time answering questions, solving problems, and maintaining order in the universe. They could be spoken to directly and couldn't pretend not to hear the speaker. Although they were gods, they were also accountable for their deeds and misdeeds. Making God invisible was a wise choice on the part of monotheists: God literally can't be bothered.

On a more disturbing note, monotheism lends itself much more readily than did earlier religions to becoming a method of mind control; an invisible but all-knowing and ever-present God sees all that you do and even knows your innermost thoughts. As a lever of behavioral control, monotheism ensures that the masses will bodily act in accordance with the rules. Any entity that controls the physical aspect of humanity also controls the mental aspect. Subjected to enough verbal repetition of an idea, people will come to believe what they are told. They may even come to believe great lies, as evidenced by the once-omnipotent power of the Nazi empire in Germany. Nazi propagandist Joseph Goebbels once said, "If you tell a lie big enough and keep repeating it, people will eventually come to believe it."[9] In this way, one leader or perceived messiah can gain control of millions of followers.

The phenomenon of divinely appointed royalty further illustrates the power of mind control. In former times, the masses considered a king to be more than a mere mortal. They bestowed upon him the added and incontestable value of having direct ties to divine power; God had placed the king on his throne, and whatever the king said and whatever decisions he made were based on this direct line to God. He was the stand-in for God on earth. The masses were as deathly afraid of angering their king as they were of incurring divine wrath. Gradually, however,

---

[9] "Joseph Goebbels Quotes," ThinkExist.com, http://thinkexist.com/quotation/-if_you_tell_a_lie_big_enough_and_keep_repeating/345877.html.

the link between God and royalty started to lose its mighty grip. The role of royalty these days has dwindled to mere figurehead for the sake of tradition. There may be some old diehards out there still, but hardly anyone today subscribes to the notion that a king is divinely appointed. It took thousands of years for this view of monarchy to change. Like everyone else, the royals have begun to show their true colors, displaying all the highs and lows of human character, including love, hate, and lust. We all know about Prince Henry's wild time in Las Vegas, courtesy of the iPhone; the news spread around the world in a split second, embarrassing good old Grandma, who had no choice but to hide.[10]

When the first notion of gods appeared, the next step for humans was figuring out how to keep them intact, not just for the present generation but for future ones as well. We can almost imagine a community leader giving a sales pitch to promote this plan, taking control of the gods-fearing people by applying multiple stripes of divinity to his own shoulders. Such a leader was able to convince his fellow villagers that he was the mediator between heaven and earth, calling himself "the son of the heavens" or "an arm of god." With his newfound followers, this pseudodivine community leader needed some kind of boost to maintain control over the people. By claiming to enjoy a special link to the gods, he assumed greater power and took the lead in already-established myths and legends. Other "arms of God" in other regions caught on to the same idea: to maintain power, they had to promote themselves continuously as being aligned with the divine. In Egypt, they picked up the title of "pharaoh," but even if they managed later to transform into gods, they still needed the support of other important figures called priests. These priests and pundits had a tumultuous relationship with pharaohs and kings throughout history. Both groups needed the other in order to succeed in deceiving and controlling the gods-fearing people.

At this point in history, no monotheistic religions existed, and neither did Hinduism. All that existed were various myths and legends.

---

[10] "Prince Harry's Wild Times," NYDailyNews.com, last modified August 22, 2012, http://www.nydailynews.com/entertainment/gossip/ prince-harry-wild-times-gallery-1.1142179.

However, all roads pointed to a common notion—that a divine act created humans to live in the world. This notion underwent many changes in its early stages, differing according to culture and geographical location. Gradually, the myths and legends settled on firmer ground, taking on a commonality and trickling down into today's religions. Ra (or Re), the sun god of Egyptian myth, gradually transformed into an all-encompassing divine being called Nebertcher,[11] the Holy Lord without limits, similar to the Almighty God of Judaism, Christianity, and Islam.

One of the most common stories among the myths and legends of all the various gods is that of the great flood. Humans needed some way to explain how they got here, and stories of surviving a great flood did just that. Norse legend asserts that the god Ragnarok became angry with humans and tried to destroy them with a massive flood.[12] The Sumerian "Epic of Gilgamesh" features a flood and a chief character named Ziusudra,[13] who, like Noah, received a heavenly message that the gods were planning to cause a deluge on earth. In a different myth, Enlil, the god of earth, wind, and fire, also wished to flood the earth.[14] In yet another, a god named Ea caused it to rain for seven nights until the world was covered with water. He then commanded Utnapishtim, the only surviving man, to build a boat and fill it with two of each creature. When the boat finally came to rest on Mount Nisir, Utnapishtim set free a dove, a swallow, and a raven to check the water levels.[15] Sounds like a dead ringer for the story of Noah's Ark! To survive, Utnapishtim was advised to build a boat, just like Noah. Interestingly, another common story from the early days involving water and survival echoes the story of Moses's infancy; it tells how babies were placed in baskets (a vessel meant as a stand-in for a boat?) and set adrift on a river like messages

[11] "Introduction, The Legend of the God Ne-ber-tcher, and the History of Creation," SacredTexts.com, http://www.sacred-texts.com/egy/leg/leg04.htm.

[12] Neil Philip, *Myths and Legends Explained* (Metro Book Publishers, 2011), 7.

[13] "Ziusudra," *Wikipedia*, last modified October 12, 2014, http://en.wikipedia.org/wiki/ziusudra.

[14] *Myths and Legends Explained*, 19.

[15] Ibid.

in bottles, in the hopes that someday someone would take them in and treasure them.[16]

In Greek mythology, Zeus also intended to drown the human race by flood; there were only two survivors, Deucalion and his wife.[17] According to a common Hindu myth, the fish Matsya, Lord Vishnu's first avatar, protected Manu, the first man, from being swept away in a flood; the fish warned Manu in advance and advised him to build an ark.[18] Myths of a great flood are common among Native American and Mexican tribes as well. A Mexican myth relates the story of Tapi,[19] who lived in a valley. The Creator told Tapi to build a boat to carry his wife and every kind of animal in pairs to safety. Everyone thought he was crazy, until it rained so hard that the valley flooded. After everyone else drowned, Tapi sent out a dove to check the water levels. All the flood stories share a few common essentials: the main characters must build a boat, save their family and the animals, end up on a mountain, send birds to check the water level, and go on creating the human race. It doesn't take much thought to recognize that many old myths and legends gradually became part of today's holy books and fixed themselves in the total narrative of the monotheistic religions.

Just like the flood stories from around the world, the various creation stories have much in common. It is possible, even likely, that present-day holy books borrowed or copied these stories from ancient myths and legends, fine-tuned them, and then claimed them as divine truth. In theogony,[20] a compilation of the genealogies of the Greek gods, the first state of the universe is Chaos (void, abyss), from which everything that exists originates. Hindu cosmology[21] describes a similar scene; in

---

[16] Tekton Apologetics, "Sargon vs. Moses," Tektonics.org, http://www.tektonics.org/copycat/sargon.php.

[17] *Myths and Legends Explained*, 24.

[18] Ibid., 110.

[19] "Other Flood Legends: Aztec," PoetPatriot.com, last modified 2010, http://www.poetpatriot.com/timeline/tmlndislegends.htm.

[20] "Theogony," Wikipedia, last modified September 12, 2014, http://en.wikipedia.org/wiki/Theogony.

[21] "Hindu Cosmology," Wikipedia, last modified October 2, 2014, http://en.wikipedia.org/wiki/Hindu_cosmology.

the Hindu beginning, there was nothing in the universe but darkness and a divine essence that removed the darkness and created the waters. The Babylonian creation story features Enuma Elish,[22] the universe in a formless state, described as a watery chaos. From this water emerged two gods, the male Apsu and the female Tiamat—and then a third deity, Mummu, the maker, where cosmogony birth begins.

Around 6 BC, Thales, "the first philosopher,"[23] proposed that everything was composed of water, which could both take and sustain life. We hear this theme echoed in the first lines of Genesis: "In the beginning, when God created the heavens and earth, the earth was a formless void. Darkness covered the face of the deep, while wind from God swept the face of the water." Before heaven and earth came into existence, there was already a beginning—darkness, wind, and water. This scene is echoed in the Qur'an also; before the first six days of creation, water and darkness already existed. Surah 21:30 states, "We made from water every living thing," and later Surah 25:54 repeats the theme: "It is He who created man from water." Water, then, is the basis of all living matter.

Part of humankind's interest in creation stories has to do with the need to feel connected to an eternal realm where the soul lives on. Humans have been chasing immortality for many thousands of years. The first humans were primarily concerned with the body in the here and now—its fatigue, disease, and eventual decline toward death. Humans most likely remembered, missed, and mourned the dead, just as they do today, only with different rituals and burial traditions. While they grieved for their loved ones, it's highly unlikely that they conceived of a soul that would cross over into an afterlife.

The birth of Egyptian civilization introduced the first notion of a soul and life after death.[24] This notion came about through the Egyptians'

---

[22] "The Babylonian Creation Story (Enuma elish)," Faculty.gvsu.edu, http://faculty.gvsu.edu/websterm/Enuma_Elish.html.
[23] "Thales," Wikipedia, last modified September 26, 2014, http://en.wikipedia.org/wiki/Thales.
[24] "Ancient Egyptian Concept of the Soul," Wikipedia, last modified June 12, 2014, http://en.wikipedia.org/wiki/Ancient_Egyptian_concept_of_the_soul.

familiarity with the process of the body's decay and decomposition. Just as they solved the problem of keeping a dead body intact, early Egyptians were determined to answer the question of "What happened to my mother?" or "Where did my sister go?" In order to make sense of death, they had to invent the concept of a soul, which to them was also a part of the body. Egyptians believed that the soul contained five parts: heart, shadow, name, personality, and vital spark.[25] To the early Egyptians, it became clear that the soul leaves the physical body after death and becomes immortal. It never dies; it just goes elsewhere.

Every human being who has experienced the heartbreak of a loved one's death understands the value of comfort. It helps to hear soothing words like "He is in a better place now" or "Someone up in heaven will take care of him." It is comforting to know that a loved one "is resting in peace" and that "his suffering has ended now." As healing occurs, grief becomes integrated into the process of life, and gradually lessens. The notion of the soul was a clever mechanism to help people in their grief process by having the dead simply move on to another place, as opposed to being inexplicably gone forever. To further the notion of life after death, Egyptian funeral practices became centered on mummification, and they buried their pharaohs with their servants and prized possessions.[26] The goal was to equip the dead person with everything he would need in the afterlife. Priests created sagas and legends about the afterlife as a continuation of the present life, with death posing as a mere interruption here in this world. The notion of an afterlife also served to encourage humans to toe the line in this life. Only the meritorious on earth would have an easy time getting to heaven. The undeserving would end up at the gates of hell.

Later scholars of the monotheistic religions redefined the soul as that which gives life to the body. As long as a person breathes, they said, he has a soul. Now, what about the recent world record holder, Gianluca

---

[25] Ibid.

[26] "Ancient Egyptian Burial Customs," *Wikipedia*, last modified September 19, 2014, http://en.wikipedia.org/wiki/Ancient_Egyptian_burial_customs.

Genoni, who held his breath for eighteen minutes and three seconds?[27] Where was Genoni's soul during that time? Did it stay inside or outside his body? He was not breathing, but other parts of his body were still functioning, independent of breath or "soul." What about people in heart surgery—their hearts detached, breathing only by artificial respiration for five or six hours? Does the human soul sit dutifully out in the waiting room, or does it remain inside the surgical arena, inspiring the surgeon? If surgery fails, does the soul say a final good-bye and drift away into eternity? If surgery succeeds, does the soul reenter the body?

In the Bible, the heart takes a front seat to the brain when it comes to thinking and analyzing human feelings. Even today, believers describe their feelings, wishes, and longings as coming from the heart. For them, the heart is the center of the human body. Think of a beautiful Valentine's Day card with the figure of a heart drawn on it, designed to capture and express all the charm, fascination, and appeal of a lover. Could we effectively swap the figure of a heart for a drawing of the brain? Of course not. The brain does not inspire the same feelings that a heart does. If you check any medical dictionary, it will explain the different roles of the brain and heart in these general terms: the heart pumps oxygen into every cell in the body, while the brain functions as the body's command center, controlling the body's every movement, voluntary and involuntary (such as breathing and heartbeat). The ancient Egyptians believed that death occurs when the "vital spark," known as Ba, leaves the body. As part of their preburial ritual, Egyptian priests would open the dead person's mouth to free this vital spark. As silly as these ancient rituals sound, we are still very much concerned with burial rituals today. Some people insist on burying a loved one in an expensive casket, dressed in formal clothes. Some wrap the loved one's body in a plain white cloth and place it in a simple pine box; some burn the body on a stack of wood; still others leave it in an open field for the vultures.

The ancient Egyptians' ideas laid the foundation for every present-day monotheistic religion. As humans expanded their awareness and assets,

---

[27] "Manufacture de Horlogerie," Blancpain.tv, http://www.blancpain.tv/video/7153913/gianluca-genoni-sets-a-new-record-160m.

their sense of gods, God, the soul, holy messengers, kings, and even the resurrection of the dead also advanced. The Bible's Daniel 12:2 asserts, "Many of those who sleep in the dust of the earth shall awake, some to everlasting life, and some to shame and everlasting contempt." These ideas were fine-tuned through the ages, changing according to cultural needs. Early biblical characters underwent changes in personality over the course of time. Even God Himself reflects these changes throughout the Old and New Testaments. For a while in the Old Testament, we see Him fairly frequently—talking with Noah in detail, sitting with Abraham at Mamre, and guiding Moses on Mount Sinai. Later on, He stopped interacting closely with humans and refrained from solving their everyday problems.

In the early chapters of the Old Testament, rewards and punishments applied to this world only. Deuteronomy 11:13 spells it out pretty clearly: in return for loving God, "He will give you the rain for your land in its season, the early rain and the later rain. You will gather it in your grain, your wine and your oil, and He will put grass in your fields for your livestock. Take care or you will be seduced into serving other gods and worshipping them. Then His anger will be rekindled against you. He will shut up the Heavens, so there will be no rain and the land will yield no fruits. Then you will perish off the land quickly, off the good land." Leviticus 26:1–4, 21–22 also delineates God's rewards for obedience and penalties for disobedience:

> You shall make for you no idols and erect no carved
> images and shall not place figure stones in your land to
> worship. You shall keep My Sabbaths; I am your Lord. If
> you keep My commandments and follow them faithfully,
> I will give you your rains in their season and the land
> shall yield its produce and the trees of the field shall yield
> their fruits. If you will not obey me, I will continue to
> plague you sevenfold for your sins. I will let loose wild
> animals against you and they will bereave you of your
> children and destroy your livestock.

Later on in the Bible, a shift occurs—from punishments pertaining to the here and now to punishments that will occur after death, once the soul has left the body. The New Testament, in particular, discusses the impact of worldly acts (or the lack thereof) on the afterlife. Jesus alludes to potential punishment in Matthew 7:21, saying, "Not everyone who says to me 'Lord, Lord' will enter the kingdom of Heaven, but only the one who does the will of my father in Heaven." In other words, simply claiming a belief in God here and now does not guarantee passage to Paradise. Jesus makes it clear that God expects people to *act* in accordance with their belief in Him; they have to live out their faith in good deeds if they want to make it to heaven. In Matthew 10:42, Jesus once again alludes to heavenly rewards for virtuous earthly deeds, saying, "And whoever gives even a cup of cold water to one of these little ones in the name of a disciple—truly I tell you, none of these will lose their reward." A more pointed example of the connection between a person's acts and his or her candidacy for entrance to heaven occurs in Matthew 12:36–37, when Jesus states, "I tell you, on the day of judgment you have to give an account for every careless word you utter; for by your words you will be justified, and by your words you will be condemned." This shift to a preoccupation with admittance to heaven stands as testimony to the shift in human thinking. When people were concerned primarily with daily survival, they wrote holy scriptures that reflected this concern. Once they had invented and developed the notion of the soul and an afterlife, the scriptures came to mention heaven and hell and what humans do to deserve each.

But God had to catch up with humanity first. He had to work through several battles with humans in the here and now before He could threaten them with eternal hell. One major battle had to do with stone figurines, carved images, and pagan gods, which posed a great challenge for Him. Humans had a choice between their familiar stone gods or the new, invisible God in the neighborhood. In the beginning, like any new kid on the block, God faced humiliation, insults, and outright assaults; He had a long, hard road ahead of Him. One thousand years after earth's creation, this new God's arrival was not going smoothly. He needed a human helper, and He found one in Noah. Although perhaps not quite up to par for the job (it turns out he had a fondness for wine), Noah "found favor in the sight of the Lord" (Gen. 6:8). He followed God's instructions obediently, which made him an easy pick. After surviving the great flood and establishing a contract with God, Noah explored his new surroundings. Genesis 9:20 tells us that Noah, a man of soil, was the first man to plant a vineyard. Unfortunately, Noah tried a little too much of the proceeds and became drunk, lying down "uncovered in his tent."

Noah's obedience was the key to his and others' survival during the great flood. But why should obedience (or disobedience) become a matter of life and death for humans? Obedience became God's number-one requirement for salvation, whereas virtue sat on the back burner. (Apparently, Noah could become inebriated as long as he obeyed God.) The requirement of obedience, then, is another lever by which God keeps people loyal to Him and controls their behavior. Humans seem to think of God as if He were Santa Claus, reminding children that they'd better be "nice" or they won't get any Christmas gifts. "Naughty" kids, you remember, get lumps of coal in their Christmas stockings. Rather than threaten them with lumps of coal, God put the fear of death into people in order to achieve His goal of total obedience. It seems that part of God's learning curve involved a stint with totalitarianism, courtesy of humanity. God's fascist tactics—specifically, having His holy messengers threaten the masses with the possibility of damnation and everlasting punishment in hell—are suspiciously similar to humans' fascist tactics. Lenin, Mussolini, and Hitler, all smashing examples of dictatorship, frequently used threats of barbaric punishment or death to ensure the loyalty of their own troops, not to mention the masses. Because people employ fascist tactics, God employs them too.

Exploring the theme of obedience a little further, we find this passage from Surah 2:285: "The Apostle believeth in what hath been revealed to him from his Lord ... 'We hear and we obey ...'" The phrase "hear and obey" sounds distinctly like an army's marching orders. And for marching orders to work efficiently, we have to have a reason to act on them. The "hear and obey" concept worked in God's favor because no one had time to think about the order or question Him. Trouble starts when one or a few out of millions raise their voices and defy orders. It occurred in the divine Kingdom of God, and it happens today in worldly kingdoms. Too often in human history, "hear and obey" orders have led to complete disasters and chaos, causing the loss of thousands of innocent human lives. Over time, humanity's pattern of thinking, pool of knowledge, and sheer capacity for reason are raising up individual and collective voices to change the current balance of social power in the hope that self-proclaimed divine kings and holy messengers will give way to the disenfranchised, impoverished, and vulnerable.

As was noted earlier, fascist tactics lead to barbaric acts. Many biblical laws and modes of punishment are now obsolete because we consider them grotesque and outrageous. Leviticus 26:29 mentions one such horrendous punishment: "And you shall eat the flesh of your sons, and the flesh of your daughters." The Qur'an also describes severe punishments. In Surah 26:91, we learn that for "those who are straying in Evil, the fire will be placed in full view." That is, those about to enter hell will first have to look into the fire and suffer the mental torture of contemplating their imminent fate. Verses 26:92–94, respectively, go on to say, "And it shall be said to them, 'Where are the gods you worshiped? Besides God? Can they help you or help themselves?'" and "'Then they will be thrown headlong into the Fire—they and those straying in Evil.'" Surah 79:39 makes its point clear: "The Abode habitat will be Hellfire for those who rebelled against God."

Earlier, according to Genesis 8:20, "God's promise to Noah," after everyone had settled down, Noah offered God a burnt sacrifice of every animal and bird. The Bible tells us that when God smelled the pleasing odor, He said in His heart, "I will never again curse the ground," and He promised Noah and his sons that He would never send such a terrible flood again. This clearly shows that just like people, God loved the smell of fresh meat (although we never hear of God eating anything). It also shows that as any human being might, God recognized that He had acted like a big, angry kid who doesn't know his own strength. Once the damage was done, God realized that He had miscalculated the flood's destructive force and regretted having caused it. He also made peace with His surviving victims, just as a human being might. Here the early writers of the Old Testament betray God's undeveloped nature—that is, they showcase early humans' rudimentary concept of God.

Let's go back to the beginning of this book for a moment and expand on one of the very first notions presented there. To understand your own religion fully, it is necessary first to investigate other religions, checking into all their beliefs and rituals and how they came to be. More than likely, it will surprise you to find that your own beliefs and rituals can appear as strange as those of other religions. You will also find that your religion shares many common liturgical events with other religions, and usually for the same reasons. Certain rites and rituals exist as a result of various nonspiritual factors, such as environment, season, geographic location, and culture. Sometimes these factors create commonalities among groups of people that otherwise would appear very different. Ultimately, belief systems exist and share commonalities because they suit a basic human need. For example, people who depend on the sea for survival may develop a belief system based on a great whale or "sea monster" that created the world. Likewise, agriculturally based people are more likely to have a belief system that features a corn or wheat god as their creator.

Therefore, when religious similarities exist among groups of people, they often can be attributed to common needs, such as the need to survive in a particular environment. Scandinavian Vikings or Norse pagans were known to build funeral pyres for their dead.[28] They created platforms for the dead, elevating the bodies above ground, and set them on fire. We might ask, "Why in the world would they do that instead of burying their dead in the ground, like so many other cultures?" But if you think about Scandinavia, it won't be long before you think of its very cold weather and even colder, often frozen, earth. The Vikings simply couldn't bury their dead; it would have taken a monumental effort to dig a grave, and bodies would have taken far too long to decompose in such frigid temperatures. Similarly, an Eskimo living in bitter cold temperatures might not quake in fear at the thought of hell; in fact, he

---

[28] "Norse Funeral," Wikipedia, last modified September 22, 2014, http://en.wikipedia.org/wiki/Norse_funeral.

might just relish the thought of a roasting fire! But a Bedouin living in the scorching climate of the Sahara Desert would no doubt find the thought of hell horribly intimidating.[29] We see here how only one of the natural elements, climate, directly shapes a given community's way of thinking and surviving, and therefore its belief systems and rituals.

The early Egyptians identified specific mountains, rivers, trees, and animals as good or bad.[30] Even today, we assign good or bad properties to certain entities; consider the "evil" black cat crossing your path, for example, or an "angry" storm cloud. Egyptians identified the Nile River as good; they came to worship it as it became the lifeline of their civilization. The good features of the world lived in tension with the bad, setting up the possibility of the existence of unknown superpowers. These powers, in turn, gradually metamorphosed into gods and goddesses. Eventually, each Egyptian village came to be "owned" by a deity whom the people worshiped according to their particular needs and circumstances. That is, each deity represented an aspect of life that concerned people: harvest, livestock, weather, wealth, etc. If a village became prosperous, people attributed its success to the correlating deity rather than the luck of the draw or human effort. Seeing the power of their neighbor's god, people in less prosperous villages wanted to join in and reap the same benefits. In this way, beliefs in certain gods spread far and wide and blended with other beliefs. Larger and better communities developed in the process.

According to accounts of Egyptian history, one of their earliest gods—Atum, "the complete one," who was thought to have created the entire universe—later became known as the sun god.[31] Atum gradually turned into the one God, El. In turn, El became Elohim, then Yahweh, then God (or Lord), and then Allah. All bear a likeness to "the complete one" or "the omnipotent, omniscient, and omnipresent." Humanity's work was to fine-tune the character of the gods, developing them successively in response to people's changing needs. This process is a

---

[29] Barbara Watterson, *Gods of Ancient Egypt* (Alan Sutton Publishing Ltd., 1996), 6.
[30] Ibid., 11.
[31] "Atum," *Wikipedia*, last modified September 26, 2014, http://en.wikipedia.org/wiki/Atum, (26 September 2014).

bit like the transformation of the first car built by Henry Ford into the highest-level car (James Bond's car, of course).

After the appearance of Atum, many other gods, and Noah, another man—Abraham—appeared on the religious stage. Rather than further developing existing gods, Abraham radicalized the nature of worship by adhering to a belief in a one-and-only God. Unlike the stone and carved gods of polytheism, Abraham's One God could not be seen, heard, or touched; people could only "see" and "hear" Him in their hearts and minds, and they could access Him internally, in their own souls. His followers no longer had to stand in front of cold, speechless statues and ask why their wishes were denied or why their prayers went unanswered. They could "talk" to God in their own minds.

The creation of an unseen God gave fresh meaning to worship and belief: you could ask anything you wished of God, and He would fulfill your dreams. However, because the new God demanded a more complex, personal relationship, your prayers might not be answered in the way you may have anticipated or wanted. The new God does not act according to anyone's time limit; He may ultimately give you what you really want (but don't know you want) in a wholly unexpected way. If by chance the new God should take fifty years to answer your prayers, don't lose hope—keep the faith, saying, "*Inshallah*" (in Arabic, "According to God's will").

And so the whole notion of faith was transformed also. People no longer turned to this new God just to ask for a good crop; they developed their faith by engaging in a relationship with God that required a turning inward to the self. It was no longer enough just to ask a deity for material items and outcomes; by engaging with God personally, humans began to improve themselves. They began striving to raise their level of personal goodness.

Abraham was the first prophet to counter idol worship, and for Muslims, worshipping idols or anything other than God is still absolutely the worst sin. Yet, as mentioned earlier, many Muslims enact a pagan rite every time they go to the Kaaba in Mecca and kiss or touch the stone there. These actions mirror the ritual performed in ancient Egypt for the god Atum, who went to the Benben stone, which was considered sacred, in the solar temple of Heliopolis.[32] Although antipagan in rhetoric, Muslim pilgrims fall head over heels to touch or kiss their holy stone. This tradition proves that the myth and ritual surrounding the god Atum continues to have an impact on Islam. Likewise, in bringing about the One God, Abraham inadvertently retained some hints of paganism; his new God still had all the old qualities of the former gods, such as absolute authority—and like the pagan priests, Abraham had the special and powerful status of holy messenger.

Muslims also inadvertently mirror another important daily ritual of ancient Egypt. When a Egyptian priest would visit the god king (stone idol) to uncover its face, he would fall on his face and kiss the ground as an act of worship. Today, Muslim believers follow the same pattern, falling on their faces five times a day to pray to Allah in the direction of the Kaaba. In addition, Egyptian people in the time of the pharaohs believed in the "evil eye," a concept still alive today. The heavenly Eye of Horus became a significant symbol of protection against the evil eye.[33] The symbol of the evil eye became popular as an amulet, and people wore this protective piece of jewelry to ward off evil spirits. You can buy evil eye jewelry today in many department stores. Some Christians wear cross necklaces in much the same way.

Pagans of Muhammad's time believed in two gods, both good, who originated in Persia. These two gods were named Isaf and Nailai, and they were believed to have settled in the hills of Safa and Marwa. During the performance of their annual rituals, pagans would run from one hill to the other, touching their idols for good luck. To appease the gods, the pagans would kiss a black stone, throw stones at Satan, and run between the statues of Isaf and Nailai. The sacrifice of animals was also a common part of their annual rituals. Muhammad continued this pagan ritual, minus the idols. The whole ceremony of Hajj is an adaptation of pagan rituals, with only minor differences. It is ironic that the Apostle of the True Faith of Islam reinvented pagan ceremonies.

---

[32] "Benben," Wikipedia, last modified September 6, 2014, http://en.wikipedia.org/wiki/Benben.

[33] "Evil Eye," *Wikipedia*, last modified September 17, 2014, http://en.wikipedia.org/wiki/Evil_eye.

In ancient times, myths and legends formed a crucial part of daily life as oral traditions; they explained social and cultural beliefs of the day. A person was raised by and indoctrinated into specific cultural norms so that he or she would accept and be accepted by the community—that is, so that he or she would conform to social standards. This was just as true for the people of Atum's (first Egyptian god) time as it was during Abraham's time. Indeed, many similarities exist between polytheistic and monotheistic religions. For example, ascending into heaven, largely thought to be the hallmark of Christianity, was a common occurrence among pagan gods long before biblical times. According to legend, Atum's son, Shu, rose into heaven on at least one occasion.[34] Which heaven the pagan Shu and the holy characters of monotheism went to, we'll never know.

Other similarities exist between ancient polytheism and monotheism. The story of Jacob's ladder seems to have its roots in ancient pagan references to a stairway to heaven. The prophet Jacob dreamed of a ladder connecting earth to heaven, upon which the angels of God ascended and descended. An Egyptian account of the sun god, Re, tells us that dead kings had a stairway by which they joined him in the afterlife. Are Jacob's ladder and Re's stairway possibly one and the same? Another similarity between polytheism and monotheism is that each of the gods was known by many names, as is the monotheistic God. The corn god (a.k.a. Osiris) was known by even more names, and when Moses asked God, "What shall I tell the Israelites in Egypt who have sent me?" God replied, "Tell the Israelites 'I am' has sent me here." Moses couldn't figure out who "I am" was, so after a while, God told him, "Tell them the God of Abraham, the God of Isaac, and the God of Jacob has sent me here" (Exod. 3:13–15). This is the same God who also goes by Yahweh and who introduced himself to Abraham as El-Shaddai[35] (God of the mountain), and to Muhammad as Allah. According to Islam, Allah has ninety-nine names, each denoting a divine property.

---

[34] *Gods of Ancient Egypt*, 33.

[35] "El Shaddai," *Wikipedia*, last modified August 31, 2014, http://en.wikipedia.org/wiki/El_Shaddai.

It is important to note here that in early civilization, the naming of things held great importance, in a way that we probably cannot quite grasp today. A name wasn't just a name; it was a claim to a being's essence. God and gods, in particular, often had secret or "unspeakable" names, due to their special and magical nature. Uttering the name of God or gods was sometimes forbidden; the name was simply too holy for human lips. The story of Isis, the most popular goddess in the Egyptian pantheon, illustrates the traditional importance of names and gaining access to them. She tried in every way imaginable, sometimes through deceit, to uncover the secret name of the great sun god, Re, as he was getting older. Eventually, she took an oath and received the name. Later in history, the Gnostics followed the same path, often spending their entire lives trying to find the secret name of God—presumably in hopes of gaining the power that the name would afford them. Even today, people call upon the name of God, sometimes formally and with purpose, and sometimes unwittingly. In performing religious rites or making solemn oaths, we say, "In the name of God." And when we stub a toe or receive good news, we often call out, "Oh God!" or "Oh my God!" Exclaiming "God!" these days isn't necessarily tied to any belief; rather, it is a common expression.

Also, a name defines a person just as a label, tag, or title does. In earlier times, surnames were based on paternal lineage, occupation, place of origin, or personal character. The name of an ordinary person typically consisted of a combination of four or five words. But as one climbed higher on the ladder of success, one's name also stretched, incorporating ten, twenty, fifty, or even ninety-nine words. Allah has ninety-nine names, and so does the prophet the world knows simply as Muhammad. His full name is: Abu-al-Qasim Muhammad Ibn Abd Allah Ibn Abd al-Muttalib Ibn Hashim, and a mixture of titles and labels brings the number of his names to ninety-nine. They include Aziz (Honorable One); Basheer (Messenger of Good News); Mustafa (Chosen One); Murtaza (the Beloved); Awal (the First); Nasir (Helper); and Ahmad (the Commendable).

Other parallels between polytheism and monotheism concern the issues of resurrection and the afterlife. First, let's look at how the notion of resurrection started. Osiris was the greatest god-king of Egypt, who ruled with compassion and concern.[36] According to legend, he taught uncivilized and cannibalistic Egyptians important skills such as growing vegetables, especially corn. As a result, he became known as the corn god. What we call Chia Pet; a terracotta figurine used to sprout chia, where the chia sprouts grow within a couple of weeks to resemble the animal's fur or hair. It is a novelty item that appears on store shelves every year around Christmas, already existed in ancient Egypt in the shape of Osiris! The Egyptians planted seeds in big clay figurines and let the Nile water them according to its cycle of flooding and ebbing. As a result of this cyclical watering, the soil of the Nile Valley would appear to die and then magically come back to life. So, too, did the "chia" god Osiris, who became a symbol of resurrection.[37] If grain can die and spring back to life, then this ability to resurrect should apply to other living beings, including the human body. From the miracle of chia-seed resurrection came the hope of everlasting life for all Egyptians.

The notion of everlasting life, in turn, changed with time. In the beginning, Egyptians took great interest in the idea, believing that the requirements for life on earth were the same for life after death.[38] And so they buried their dead with clothing, drinks, medicines, and even food. (As a shortage of food was the biggest obstacle for the living, they reasoned, so it must be for the dead.) They made sure the dead had everything they would need in the afterlife. Monotheistic believers took these same ideas and developed them in their own way. Again, using basic Egyptian beliefs, monotheists adhered to the notion of the "soul" but fashioned one that can survive death independent of the material goods of this world. This shift in the understanding of the soul made packing for the afterlife obsolete and made the burial ritual a lot easier for everyone, dead and alive.

Yet another example of the ancients' impact on today's religions is reflected in the observation of certain dietary laws. In ancient Egypt, pigs were considered unclean and were not served as food. They were

[36] "Osiris," *Wikipedia*, last modified October 8, 2014, http://en.wikipedia.org/wiki/Osiris.
[37] *Gods of Ancient Egypt*, 56.
[38] "Ancient Egyptian Burial Customs."

kept isolated from the rest of the community to limit swine-to-person contamination. Later on in history, Jews and Muslims followed the same trend of forbidding the consumption of pig meat, making the ban part of religious law. The Egyptians had already figured out dangers of eating poorly cooked pork and had already established many other spiritual beliefs and rituals that laid the groundwork for the future, monotheistic God and His messengers. If it weren't for all the hard work by Egyptians early on in history, the monotheists would have had a much harder time trying to establish all their rules and religious beliefs. The only thing the God of Abraham, Moses, Jesus, and Muhammad had to do was find the pagan–Egyptian recipe book for myths, legends, and beliefs, add or subtract a few spices—and voila! They'd made their own recipe books.

Another element of monotheism that takes its cue from the pagan past is the practice of religious frenzy. We have only to look at the cult of Dionysus as a clear example of ecstatic worship. Their form of religious frenzy revolved around debauchery and excess of every kind. The Roman god Bacchus, known as "the liberator," was a noted cult figure whose worship included drinking and dancing and what we would call "free love." His followers often arrived at religious events dressed in ivy and dripping in honey.[39] A precedent had already been set, then, to include various physical indulgences, including intoxication, in worship. In the Old Testament, religious frenzy may not have involved these sorts of material excesses, but those in a state of frenzy certainly fell under the influence of music and entered dissociative or trancelike states. The first book of Samuel 8:5 tells the story of how this practice came about in biblical times: "The elders of Israel gathered and came to Samuel and said to him, 'Give us a king to govern us like other nations.'" Samuel was a respected priest and judge of his time. After getting the Lord's approval, he reluctantly gave them permission to have a king. He started setting the stage to anoint Saul as king of Israel, giving Saul certain instructions and then saying, "After you come to Gibeath-Elohim, a Philistine garrison, you will meet a band of prophets with harps, tambourine, and flutes,

---

[39] "Dionysus," *Wikipedia*, last modified October 8, 2014, http://en.wikipedia.org/wiki/Dionysus.

who will be in a prophetic frenzy. The spirit of the Lord will control you, and you will be in a prophetic frenzy with them and turned into a different person."

*Frenzy* is defined as a temporary state of madness, violent agitation, and intense, wild motion. This state of mind is common among followers of Islamic Sufism and evangelical Christianity. They enter into a trancelike state in order to experience an intensity of the presence of God. A trancelike state, however, does not necessarily denote the presence of God. Modern audiences have been known to fall into "frenzied" states at the sight of Michael Jackson's moonwalk, for example. People at rock concerts often lose their inhibitions and behave in ways they normally would not, sometimes taking drugs or drinking to excess. They might cry and scream, lose control of their movements, jump up on stage to be with the rock star, or get into altercations with others in the audience. It can look a bit like bacchanalian worship! Again, we see the same elements of mind control here that we discussed earlier. People who lose themselves in religious or other kinds of rapture are more easily controlled and persuaded to do whatever bidding the elders (show producers) demand. Today, people give hundreds and even thousands of dollars to TV preachers while in a compromised state of mind. Here's where religion shows its dark side; it can be used for criminal purposes just as surely as can a gun held to another's head. Elderly and emotionally unstable people have been known to give up their entire life savings to these TV preachers, unaware at the time of the consequences of their actions. For the preachers, it's all about having power over others in order to make money.

An ancient equivalent of the TV preacher is the high priest. Around the time that the Jews were exiled from Judah, the importance of the high priest was increasing. For these exiled Jews, a leadership vacuum existed, as they no longer had a king to serve as a link between themselves and God. High priests hurried to fill the gap, inventing their own "power tools" to indicate their proximity to God's authority. They claimed to interpret the will of God using what was known as the "breast plate"—a pouch containing twelve stones representing the twelve tribes of Israel. The high priest wore the pouch on his heart when he entered the temple. These precious stones, called Urim and Thummim, gave priests the authority of decision making. At the time, people had blind faith in these stones and accepted the high priests' decisions as the will of God. How bizarre does this belief seem today, after two thousand years? Yet it's no less bizarre than many beliefs and practices that appear today and will also appear two thousand years from now.

From the beginning of biblical times, kings and priests fought a constant tug-of-war to gain the more powerful position. It is startling to think that holy priests, who were supposed to serve as links between God and the community, would struggle so fiercely for a worldly, political throne. We see an example of this in the dynamic rift among emperors, popes, and bishops. In Western Europe pope was head of the Christian church and believed that all religious officials (and royal) officials should answer to him. The Eastern Europe church was controlled by bishops and disagreed with Pope Leo IX, causing a split between two churches. His Holiness excommunicated the Eastern Church leaders. Those who supported Pope Leo became Roman Catholic, making the pope the strongest and most powerful figure of his time, but at the same time, the pope's problems with the kings grew more intense. The pope was the head of the Christian church in Europe, and people revered him greatly. When the Roman Empire collapsed, causing a political vacuum, people still looked to the pope for guidance. This gave him an excellent opportunity to increase his authority and power by also fulfilling the role of king, and living like one. In England and France, kings inherited thrones for generations. In Rome, popes were stronger than kings, causing kings to seek their approval. The people accepted their government as a Holy Roman Empire.

Few decades later the political power struggle started again between Emperor Henry IV and new Pope Gregory VII. Their disagreement was, who had the right to appoint church officials. The emperor Henry IV wanted to include bishops in the church, and Pope Gregory VII disagreed. Emperor Henry IV took a gamble and asked his bishops to excommunicate Pope Gregory, which backfired, getting him excommunicated instead. Emperor Henry wanted to apologize to Pope Gregory, but His Holiness was in no mood to talk, and did not respond. The Emperor stayed barefoot for days outside the Pope's home to show humility and ask forgiveness. When things returned to normal, Emperor Henry waited for his turn and went back to Rome. He forced Pope Gregory into exile. For two supposed holy men, what an example of the lust for power! This same struggle became the norm between popes and kings for hundreds of years.

Abraham, Moses, Jesus, and Muhammad were not the only leaders who introduced the notion of a monotheistic God to their communities. Around 1350 BC, King Amenphis IV, one of the pharaohs, espoused the worship of one God in Egypt: Aton, the sun god. (Note the likeness between "Aton" and "Atum.") The idea was short-lived, however, and abandoned after the king's death. The Qur'an contains no reference to Pharaoh King Amenphis IV, although it mentions pharaohs more than one hundred times—mostly in a demeaning manner, as if they were all evil. Out of all the pharaohs, the Qur'an names one righteous character, a pharaoh's wife. Surah 66:11 states, "And God sets forth, as an example to those who believe, the wife of Pharaoh. She said: 'O Lord! Build for me, in nearness to Thee, a mansion in the Garden and save me from Pharaoh and his doings.'" In exchange for nearness to God, the righteous wife of Pharaoh asked for nothing less than a mansion! Just like any human, God can get friendly with the enemy of His enemy.

In all the accounts of God's appearances in all the holy books, He never takes on any physical features or shape. We have to use our imaginations to fill in the blanks. Only the prophet Jacob claims to have seen God in any meaningful way. In Genesis 32:28, Jacob says, "For I have seen God face-to-face, and yet my life is preserved." However, he never describes God in any detail, despite having wrestled with Him all night on one occasion, to the point where Jacob's hip joint became dislocated.

The question remains: How is it that when we are gifted with vision and have such amazing brains to work with, we can never see God? And why is it that, when we need to see and hear God most, He picks one apostle to convey His messages, with all kinds of question marks attached? How odd it is that here on earth we do our utmost to communicate, connect, and converse with God through all His approved means, yet we never see Him. We pray, offer animal sacrifices, fast, and travel thousands of miles to visit various houses of God, but all our efforts are in vain. But the instant we die, God will appear. Surah 3:143 "You did indeed wish for death before you met him: now you see him with your own eyes." All nevertheless is a deception? But the moment we die, we will be able to see Him! This sequence of events seems to be in reverse order. My humble advice to people, offered from my corner of the universe, is that instead of looking for vague, theoretical signs of God's existence from a handpicked 124,000 messengers, they should ask God to come down to earth and give us proof. Without it, isn't His existence hard to grasp? Why should people settle for an invisible God in real life? Why give such importance to invisibility? One answer, of course, is that humans hold closely to a skewed concept of God for many reasons—among them the fear of death and the hope that after a life of wrangling intensely and unkindly with other humans, there might be a place of peace and quiet.

# 2

## THE AGRICULTURAL REVOLUTION GAVE BIRTH TO THE MEANING OF MARRIAGE

This chapter touches on the complex subject of human wickedness, and how religion attempted to intervene in people's everyday life following the Agricultural Revolution. From day one, humans learned to survive in part by finding shortcuts, cheating, and stealing. Humans lived as hunter-gatherers for a long time. Early hunters needed roughly eight square miles of land to feed one person. It was a hard, cumbersome job. Prior to the Agricultural Revolution, order existed in daily routines, which dictated people's function and place in society. In the early mornings, the men went hunting; in the evenings, the women cooked; and late at night, everyone shared meals and swapped adventurous stories of the day. The elders set strict rules for the community. The development of agriculture transformed human life forever. People discovered how to plant seeds and grow crops to feed 150 humans in only five square miles. They knew that a wheat seed would produce only wheat, not rice. They could organize their food and plan their food for the future. The human population grew, bringing more and more humans together. This boom in population profoundly affected daily social events. Without the previous tight-knit communities ruled by elders, social behavior lacked boundaries and changed for the worse. Something had to be done.

Enter: Frank and Harry. They were the best of friends. They lived happily with their respective female partners in a small neighborhood by the river. They lived by a code of honor, shared their daily adventures, and trusted each other. When Frank's partner gave birth to their first baby, Frank was ecstatic, but soon his happiness turned into shock and dismay. There was a suspiciously strong physical likeness between Harry and Frank's new bundle of joy—a resemblance too strong to ignore. Frank soon remembered the agricultural lesson that a wheat seed does not produce rice. He realized that Harry had broken his trust and sown his seed in an unlawful place. That same night all hell broke loose, and the village's first war started. It began with heated exchanges and disintegrated into chaos. Wise old men recognized the problem: Frank and his female partner had no formal agreements with each other regarding their social, financial, and personal family matters. So the elders drew up a simple plan for all couples living together to formalize their arrangement as a promise in the presence of their friends. The eldest man of the village would certify it.

At first, marriage was not a necessity, but it slowly became a need in the early ages of progress. The purpose of marriage was to promote the orderly and respectful social union of a man and a woman (and also to promote childbirth and keep track of lineage). Slowly, the code of marriage spread to all societies, cultures, communities, and religions. Various tribes added their own spin to the happy union of man and woman. Later on, religious leaders formalized the marriage process. Codes of marriage had to pass through several levels of church, mosque, and temple approval. Marriage became a holy union, a holy rite, and was given strict guidelines and meaning. Most important, social events such as marriage now required religious approval.

Each religion began to have a more intense impact on people's daily life, and so did the code of marriage. At one point, marrying into other religions was forbidden. Muslim men were not to marry anyone who was not a monotheist; in Surah 2:221 of the Qur'an, Allah admonishes men not to "marry unbelieving woman idolaters until they believe." The Bible's Ezra 9:11 also denounces religiously mixed marriages: "The land that you are entering to take over is a land unclean with the pollutions of the people of the land. Do not give your daughters to their sons; neither take their daughters for your sons." After thousands of years, however, the definition of marriage has changed and broadened. Society, by and large, has redefined marriage and broken old barriers of beliefs regarding race and gender. Nevertheless religious leaders and holy books typically had a short and handy answer to any question regarding the practice of marriage: "God said so." This became the response to every challenge to religious law, and eventually, people came to repeat it over and again, no matter how valid or logical an opposing argument might be in favor of changing or reinterpreting the law.

So marriage became one answer to human wickedness. Creating religiously sanctioned practices that become legalized social ritual certainly served as a lever of moral restraint. But there was still much to be done to define marriage codes and rituals according to social, cultural and religious edicts.

# 3

## PEOPLE LOVE MYTHS,
## MIRACLES, AND MAGIC

Genesis 6:5 tells us that the "Lord saw the wickedness of humankind was great in the earth, and that every inclination of the thoughts of their hearts was evil continually." The time from Adam to Noah spanned a thousand years. The earth was fresh, and humans represented a "tabula rasa"—a clean slate. God busily set the stage to promote His plan for all His characters, and His audience too. How humans turned dishonest and corrupt in such a short period of time is a mystery. Of course, there is always Satan to explain it.

Satan, one of God's favorite angels, directly rebelled against Him by refusing to follow one of His commands. He showed up in the Garden of Eden as a snake, defying God again by luring Eve into eating fruit from a forbidden tree. Eve, in turn, persuaded Adam to eat the apple. And so a small bite of fruit made sinners of all future generations of humans. At this point, God apparently took a two-thousand-year break, and then He sent Jesus to take care of everyone's sins. From the time of Noah on, hundreds of holy messengers had preached, but none could live up to being a messiah in the true biblical sense like Jesus could. God also gave Jesus (who was His kid, after all) the power of making miracles. The human brain cannot help but be fascinated by superhumans and their powers, especially when they defy the laws of nature. We call their powers and abilities "miracles." People love to see, hear, and believe in miracles. Every few years, for example, we hear about the appearance of the Virgin Mary in South America, notably in the most devoted Roman Catholic countries. Below is a list of some well-known modern-day miracles:

- The Crying Statue Miracle: In December 1992, a Catholic, working-class Chilean woman saw tears of blood coming out of a small statue of the Virgin Mary.[40]
- The Hindu Milk Miracle: Journalists held a milk-filled spoon to the gods and watched as the milk disappeared.[41]
- The Eggplant Miracle: In 1996 in Bolton, United Kingdom, Mrs. Ahmad Patel foresaw a miracle in a dream after buying an eggplant from a local shop. After slicing the eggplant, she saw seeds formed in the shape of the Muslim phrase "Ya-Allah."[42]
- The Buddhist Miracle: Burmese religious flocked by the thousands to see a multicolored beam streaming from a Buddhist monastery about a hundred miles from Rangoon. The monk who gave sermons there had been known for his lengthy speeches; listeners needed to remain still for hours with their eyes closed. When he changed his technique, shortening his sermon to twenty minutes and requiring listeners to keep their eyes wide open, with no blinking, some followers saw the remnants of Buddha and rainbow colors coming from the monastery roof.[43]

Strikingly, followers see only their *own* faith symbols during these miracles. Why does the Muslim phrase "Ya-Allah" not appear in the eggplants of Catholics or Jews? If we are all children of one God, why doesn't God show miracles of one faith to followers of other faiths?

Some "miracles" were based simply on a misunderstanding of

---

[40] "Bleeding Image of Mary, Chile," VisionsofJesusChrist.com, http://www.visionsofjesuschrist.com/weepingstatuesandicons.htm.

[41] "Hindu Milk Miracle," *Wikipedia*, last modified October 5, 2014, http://en.wikipedia.org/wiki/Hindu_milk_miracle.

[42] "Miracle Aubergine with Ya-Allah," IslamAwareness.net, last modified December 1996, http://www.islamawareness.net/Miracles/miracle_aubergine.html.

[43] "Buddhist Miracles," Miracles.mcn.org, http://miracles.mcn.org/m-image.html.

natural events. In the Qur'an, the story of a proud, wealthy man named Qarun, who credited himself and not God for his wealth, demonstrates what the people of that time interpreted as divine justice, as noted in Surah 28:81: "Then We caused the earth to swallow him up and his house …" The Bible's Numbers 16:32, in reference to certain sinful people, describes how the "earth opened its mouth and swallowed them." Today, we call this rather dramatic occurrence a "sinkhole"—a natural depression in the earth caused by the removal of underground soil by water. Sinkholes can develop slowly over time, causing cracks in the earth as a warning sign—or they can occur suddenly, making the earth look as if it has magically disappeared. The people who witnessed the above incidents had no knowledge of geology to explain sinkholes. Believers were so captivated by the "miracle" of disappearing earth that they held themselves responsible, believing it to be a sign of God's wrath. It didn't occur to them to get mad at God for causing such devastation in the land!

Miracles often occur during natural and man-made disasters. When any human being or object survives a horrendous event, their survival becomes a "miracle." Take the example of an airplane carrying one hundred passengers from New York to Los Angeles that crashes, leaving two survivors. People declare their survival an act of divine mercy rather than blaming God for the ninety-eight lives lost; what they think of as divine mercy and miracles might be nothing more than the luck of the draw. The real, mind-boggling miracle would be if God were to reassemble the crashed plane, resurrect the dead, and deliver all one hundred passengers safely to LAX. Could God make this happen? Judging from the record, it seems to be a challenge for God to produce proof of miracles. I am inclined to believe that a true miracle has not happened in the past and will not happen in the future. It seems that whenever we can't find a logical reason for an unusual event, a miracle has occurred. Take a Polaroid camera to any part of the world where technology is still woefully rudimentary or nonexistent, find a willing person, take his picture, and hand it to him. Undoubtedly, the camera will at first appear to be a "magic box." Let him take loads of pictures of everyone in his village. Later, show him the technique and mechanics of the camera, and it will become a normal box. After a while, the thrill of the box will vanish, and soon it will be collecting dust. That's how our human brain works with miracles.

Imagine positioning Moses, Jesus, and Muhammad at different points around the globe for a show of modern miracles. Tell Jesus to take a selfie and send it to Moses via the Internet. Tell Moses to wake up Muhammad by cell phone and say, "A picture of me and Jesus will appear on your computer screen in a minute." Muhammad's response would be "Moses! Are you as divine as God now?" "Maybe better," Moses would respond. "My Yahweh only taught me the simple trick of throwing a rod that turned into a snake in Pharaoh's court." The story of the rod turned snake appears silly compared to this "miracle" of modern science, the Internet. Today thousands of people, young and old, walk around with palm-sized boxes full of modern miracles. Ironically, they use these boxes to see, talk, and hear, but they can't see another person coming toward them only a few feet away!

People are more prone to seek out miracles during times of immense difficulty or challenge. For example, the story of Superman found remarkable success during the Great Depression of the 1930s. Everybody needed a hero at that point in history. As poor as they were, people scraped together enough money to buy Superman comic books, enthralled by his powers and good works. When Superman movies were made, people flocked to the cinema to forget about life for a while, paying a good day's wages to let Superman fix everything. And fix it he did. Superman took on the role of social activist, fighting crooked businesspeople and politicians. He even taught slumlords a lesson by demolishing run-down tenements. A champion of social causes and a friend to the American people, Superman represented the great hope that one day life would get better. Most Americans today are familiar with Superman's description: "Faster than a speeding bullet, more powerful than a locomotive, able to leap tall buildings in a single bound."

It is possible that Superman's character was partially influenced by the story of Moses. Superman's "real" name was "Kal-El," which echoes the Hebrew term for "voice of God." The suffix "El" means God. The supermen of biblical times, however, may not have had purely altruistic motives; it seems that, to some degree, they set themselves up as idols—and in Moses's case, dragged a group of six hundred thousand people to wander aimlessly in a barren desert. If Moses came back today and repeated the same performance, he would have no more than six hundred followers left at the end of his journey.

Good mysteries can appear close in nature to miracles; they amaze and astound even the cleverest people. All the best biblical supermen had an element of mystery to them, to varying degrees. So did God Himself, for that matter. When God sent His holy messengers to coax the human race into believing in Him, it's no surprise that they used a great deal of mystery to convey the nature of God. They had to mystify the image of God in order to arouse curiosity and awe. Understanding that this sense of mystery is really a smoke screen for a political campaign is a bit like watching *The Wizard of Oz* for the first time and realizing that the Great and Powerful Oz is just a little old man behind a curtain.

# 4

## PARALLELS BETWEEN GOD AND HUMAN BEHAVIOR

Much of the text of the holy books, therefore, is hard to understand—that is, "mysterious"—which is odd, considering the importance of their messages. We would expect these texts to be thoroughly precise and as detailed as the US Code of Federal Regulations. Divided into fifty sections, this code contains 169,301 pages and is updated every calendar year. Combined, the Bible and the Qur'an contain roughly 1,500 pages, and their language is often vague, requiring readers to use their imaginations to interpret them. Take, for example, the following verse from the biblical story of the creation of Adam: "He breathed in him something of His part." The word *something* is defined as an object that cannot be specifically designated and can be used in many abstract ways. Let's suppose that God indeed breathed "something" into the first human. My first question is "What was this ambiguous, imagined 'thing' breathed by an invisible being?" followed quickly by my second question: "Does God really have breath the way humans do? If so, how does He breathe? And what does 'His part' mean?" My third question is this: "Why would God start His human project off so well, only to have Adam defy His laws so soon and become a sinner?" Perhaps there was some trace of pollution in the "something" that God breathed into Adam—something that caused devilish symptoms in him and in future generations.

In trying to make sense out of all the above, let's take a look at what

God says about judging His handiwork. Then let's go further and assess God's performance as Judge, and see what we can learn about His nature. It seems that to disagree with God about His handiwork is to be His enemy. Qur'an 5:47, states, "Let the people of the Gospel judge what God hath revealed therein. If any do fail to judge by the light of what God hath revealed, they are no better than those who rebel." We're already on God's bad side before we begin! God almost sounds like a dictator, trying to sway people's opinion about His revelations His way. The first part of the surah seems reasonable and rational. The second part raises a red flag, because it sounds like human words. We appoint a judge to evaluate with fairness, neutrality, and independence. In the sports arena, a referee must give his honest decision, independent of the fans' or the players' opinions, and certainly without considering what God might think. What good is a judge who can be swayed by popular opinion or have his arm twisted by higher authorities?

God may have started out on the right foot, but as we have seen, He quickly begins thinking and acting like a human being. Where did He get the bright idea to "make humankind in Our image?" (Gen. 1:26). And yet God wants to be the only one, as evidenced by Surah 6:19 of the Qur'an: "Can you possibly bear witness that beside God there is another God? Say: 'Nay! I cannot bear witness!' Say: 'But in truth He is the one God.'" God demands this singular devotion, and in the same breath He brushes aside any critiques, instantly dictating that we accept His opinion without any reason other than "Say: 'Nay! I cannot bear witness!' Say: 'But in truth He is the one God.'" In Surah 6:37, we see that "God has power to send down a sign. But most of them understand not." Here we have God complaining and pointing fingers, just like a human being jabbing a finger at his neighbor on the other side of the fence. God does not seem to understand that the "power to send down a sign" is not the end of the story. If humans can't interpret God's signs and His obscure network of revelations, then why wouldn't He add a few more IQ points to the human brain to enable us to understand? It's simple: if some kids don't understand a lesson, the teacher has the responsibility of changing the teaching strategy until they do understand.

It is questionable, however, whether God really does want us to understand. He seems to have second thoughts in Genesis 3:22: "The Lord said, 'See, the man has become like us, knowing good and evil. Now he might reach out his hand and take also from the tree of life, and eat, and live forever.'" When Adam first ate from the tree of knowledge, God appeared shocked and alarmed—almost panicky, like a mighty monarch who knows his rival is ready to challenge him at close range. Knowing good from evil is part of the basic fabric of human life. Wouldn't it be better for everyone to understand this—and wouldn't it be easier on God too? Why is human knowledge of good and evil such a concern to God? Maybe God intentionally wants to keep the human race in the shadows. In His progressive sequence of panic, God looks at the other tree, the Tree of Life, and perhaps imagines His future hanging in the balance with the prospect of everlasting humans. God's simple solution and divine justice is to send Adam "forth from the Garden of Eden to till the ground from which he was taken." Let's put this situation in the context of a human father and his children. Let's say he puts a jar of cookies in the middle of the room, knowing it is harmful for his kids. The moment the kids are caught with their hands in the cookie jar, the dad throws the kids out of the room instead of removing the cookie jar.

Next we see God's irascible side again. In Surah 2:258 of the Qur'an, God says, "Of those who reject faith the patrons are the Evil ones." So we're either with God or against Him? Does rejecting faith mean an automatic ticket to hell? Why do we have to be labeled evil just for not going along with God? This is the same God that didn't want human beings to know good from evil. Let's go back to the Garden of Eden, to the scene where Adam has just finished his first bite of the forbidden fruit and is about to be tempted to eat another one. Adam's first bite of fruit raised a red flag for God. The second bite from the Tree of Life would have made Adam as immortal as God; Adam and future generations would have never died and would have been full of knowledge, just like God. If the human race had become as good and everlasting as God, no crimes ever would have occurred—and there would have been no starvation, wars, or plagues either. No one would have needed the Ten Commandments. There would have been no hell and therefore no need to send Moses, Jesus, or Muhammad to this world. The earth would have been the perfect place to live forever. Was it a blunder on God's part to throw Adam and Eve out of Eden?

God seemed to know that, if endowed with godlike qualities, Adam would have flatly refused to be thrown out of the Garden of Eden. God became highly possessive of those two trees—just like we humans become protective of our nearest and dearest property, hard-earned money, prophets, religion, leaders, and friends. Perhaps the two mysterious trees in the Garden of Eden were God's lifeline. Perhaps He achieved all His supernatural qualities from the fruits of those two trees. Did the trees in Eden hold the key to producing godlike beings? Why did he have the trees at all, if no one could share their fruits? The sole beneficiary of these mysterious trees was God Himself. That could be the only reason God protected them so passionately: they held the secret of His strength, just like kryptonite gave Superman his mighty powers.

In Surah 6:59 of the Qur'an, we learn that "He knows whatever there is on earth and sea ... Not a leaf does fall but with His knowledge." Are we really supposed to believe that of all the gazillions of leaves hanging on the billions of trees in this world, not one falls without God knowing it? The Qur'an is asking us to believe in God's omniscience. The above verse sounds poetic and metaphorical, but Genesis 3:8 seems to refute God's omniscience. Adam and Eve "heard the sound of the Lord God walking in the garden at the time of the evening breeze, and the man and his wife hid themselves from the presence of the Lord God. But the Lord called to the man and said, 'Where are you?'" God really had to ask Adam his whereabouts? Later, in Genesis 3:11, God asks, "Who told you that you are naked? Have you eaten from the tree of which I commanded you not to eat?" Likewise, when Cain kills his brother, Abel, the Lord asks Cain where Abel is. If God were omnipresent and omniscient, He would have no need to ask these questions. If God had a problem finding the only two human beings in His own Garden, how does He manage a garden of seven billion people today? At least there's one question God will never have to ask a particular crowd again: folks at the nude beach! God accepted nakedness in the Garden of Eden, so frequenting nude beaches in this world should not be a question of morality.

Another passage that refutes God's omniscience and omnipresence is from Genesis 18:20–21: "How great is the outcry against Sodom and Gomorrah and how grave their sin! I must go down and see whether they have done altogether according to the outcry that has come to me; and I will know." When God says "I must go down," He suggests that He was "up" somewhere. Being either up or down does not signify omnipresence. Up or down is not everywhere. Also, in order to know what was going on, He had to change locations. If God were truly omniscient and omnipresent, His location wouldn't matter. It's no wonder humans are confused by God's revelations. We're told one thing in one holy book and something different in another. At any rate, in Surah 3:179 of the Qur'an, we learn the hard truth that God isn't much interested in showing or explaining too much, anyway: "He separates what is evil from what is good. Nor He will disclose to you the secrets of the unseen." Usually, believers explain that humans can't figure out God's messages because the human brain is not capable of understanding the divine. In this case, however, we're just told that we're not going to know the secrets of unseen. Period. God's refusal to reveal these secrets sounds a bit like "taking the Fifth"—that is, it sounds like He's calling on the Fifth Amendment of the US Constitution, which was originally designed to guard against confessions based on torture. The purpose and intent of the Fifth Amendment were fair and humane. As we all know, however, the average mobster typically pleads the Fifth, which often signifies guilt, or at least that you have something to hide. God is a step ahead of the Fifth Amendment; He not only hides the "secrets of the unseen" but chooses His own apostles (witnesses).

# 5

## GOD AND PROPHETS ARE
## INSECURE AT TIMES

One would think that humans would have been living in a peaceful, loving, and harmonious environment after their close call with the great flood, Noah's intervention, and the introduction of Moses to the people. But that is not how life turned out. After a long, humiliating journey, and after suffering forty years of physical torture in the desert at the hands of Pharaoh, the Israelites saw what looked like relief in Moses. What they really saw, however, was a mirage Moses created; as we will see, he was good at employing tricks to secure power. God helped Moses create this mirage in the valley of Mount Sinai. The Israelites dug in their heels, ready to conquer the land of milk and honey, as they'd been promised would happen, but their determination did not last long. Clashes and conflicts soon arose while Moses was up on the mountain with God. In Moses's absence, the Israelites fell apart and began worshiping idols again, incurring God's wrath. In Deuteronomy 32:51, He says, "Moses and Aaron broke faith with Me among the Israelites at the water of Maribath-Kadish, in the wilderness of Zen, by failing to uphold my holiness among Israelites," and He tells both men, "Although you may view the land from a distance, you shall not enter it; the land I am giving to the Israelites." Poor Moses, who gave his entire life for his belief in Yahweh and the Promised Land, ended up shut out. All he could do was peep through a window from Mount Nebo, wishing he could set foot on the other side. God let Moses die before he could get to the Promised Land.

He wasn't the only prophet to get a rough deal. When told by God in Genesis 17:10 that "every male among you shall be circumcised," Abraham was the first one to start hacking away at his private parts. This was part of the covenant God made with him in Genesis 15:18 on that day the Lord made a covenant with Abram, saying, "To your descendants I give this land, from the river of Egypt to the great river, the river Euphrates"—property in exchange for self-mutilation? Abraham's followers kept their side of the bargain by enforcing circumcision, but God did not keep His side. Without a doubt, however, Jesus got the shorter end of the stick. Jesus (God's Son, mind you) cried out loud on the cross with these last words: "Eloi, Eloi, lema sabachthani?" (Mathew 27:46). In English, this means, "My God, my God, why have you abandoned me?" Surah 14:47 of the Qur'an tells us, "Never think that God will fail His Apostles in His promise." God actually seems to have great difficulty keeping His promises. We've already seen how He snatched away Moses's cherished dream of entering the Promised Land. The spirit of Moses must be still peeping through the window from Mount Nebo.

Finally, the Israelites settled down in the Promised Land and felt comfortable, strong, and prosperous in their trades. Then the time came for them to lead the way and flex their muscles in the region. They wanted to extend their territories and rule their nearby neighbors. The Israelites had found their one lucky God named Yahweh, who had given them success on every battlefield. They had every reason to put Him on the highest pedestal, and they came to feel a sense of security and superiority. Now was the right time to push Yahweh down the throats of those who followed rival gods like Baal, El, and Elohim.

When Moses died, he passed the prophetic baton to Joshua, who then held the title of helper to Moses. The prophet Joshua executed thirty-one kings, leaving only half a dozen unconquered by the time he reached old age. The lucky few lived in a territory of about three hundred by one hundred miles. So each king had an average territory of about thirty-one square miles in which he could impose his own beliefs, customs, and gods. Each territory remained foreign to the next, and each followed its own rigid laws. Joshua was about to end all that. He rallied his troops, saying, "I therefore command you: 'Be strong and fearless; do not be frightened or dismayed, for the Lord your God is with you wherever you go'" (Josh. 1:9). And so the Israelites went out again to conquer other kingdoms. Joshua 6:21 tells how "they devoted to destruction by the edge of the sword all in the city, both men and women, young and old, oxen, sheep, and donkeys." Joshua 8:24 and 10:28, respectively, show the continued bloodshed in Ai and Makkedah under God's command: "When Israel had finished slaughtering all the inhabitants of Ai in the open wilderness they chased them. All Israel returned to Ai, and attacked them by the edge of the sword till all fell. Joshua stretched out his sword, destroyed all the inhabitants of Ai," and "Joshua took Makkedah on that day. He struck it and its king with the edge of the sword. He destroyed every person in it; he left no one remaining." Then, just to finish things off in style, "Joshua said to the chiefs of the warriors, 'Come near and put your feet on the necks of these kings.' And afterwards Joshua struck them down and put them to death and hung them on five trees" (Josh. 10:24).

Joshua looks like the grand butcher of all butchers under the command of the Lord, God of Israel. He burned the cities and all the residents of those cities: men and women, young and old, and even the kings. Does Joshua then deserve credit as a biblical hero? After all, "It was the Lord's doing to harden the Israelites' enemies' hearts so they would come against Israel in battle. So they might be destroyed, just as the Lord had commanded Moses" (Josh. 1:9). Yahweh was winning the Israelites' hearts; they obeyed, worshiped, and followed his promptings. In return, He gave them victory after victory.

Eventually, everyone got the message of Joshua: "If you abandon the Lord and serve foreign gods then He will turn and do you harm and consume you" (Josh. 24:20). As the victories of kings began to slip away, it was easy for kings and tribal leaders to blame their people for disowning their own gods. Despite "reasons" for success or failure, like obedience or disobedience to God, there comes a time when those at the top naturally fall from that position, beginning to show signs of decline and fatigue. All the great empires throughout history peaked and then declined without any help from religion, Yahweh, God, or Allah. The only difference with religion in the picture is that mighty empires propagated the myth of religion and mediator god-kings to keep a heavy-handed grip on innocent people.

After Joshua's reign, Judah of Israel was the next to take command. It was up to him to finish the job, as there were still parts of Canaan left unconquered. Once again, the Lord said, "Judah shall go up to fight against Canaanites. I give the land into his hand" (Judg. 1:2). Nowhere does God mention the exact procedure by which Judah should take over leadership; nor does He specify how Judah will care for the welfare of his followers. Did God utter these exclusive words in the presence of a prominent community group? Or did Judah, like others before him, proclaim himself leader based on a personal divine message? Perhaps as the one with the mightiest sword, he thought he was the best man for the job, but he insisted instead on taking it because "the Lord said so." How could the people know they were hearing the right message and getting the right messenger? People just didn't ask these kinds of questions in biblical times, because religion served as the crux of human regulation. They dutifully accepted the truth as it was handed to them by those in positions of religious authority.

# 6

## CIVILIZATIONS ARE OFTEN ON A ROLLER-COASTER RIDE

A 2007–2008 Gallup Poll implemented in several European countries asked the question "Does religion occupy an important role in your life?" The results were as follows: In the Scandinavian countries, 80 percent of respondents said no. Respondents in France, the United Kingdom, and Holland said no 70 percent of the time, in Italy 26 percent of the time, and in Rumania 18 percent of the time. These countries are known for their excellent social welfare programs. They have enough food for the poor, and at the same time, they show less reliance on religious institutions. On the contrary, underdeveloped areas with the most poverty and social problems, like Africa and Asia, tend to be the most religious. The people of poor countries have not disowned God, but somehow they suffer the most. God must be at it again: changing sides, disowning the underdogs, and favoring people who don't love Him as much.

In many parts of the world, the saying goes that "money can't buy you happiness," which is partly true. But neither does poverty. Money's biggest value is that it buys life's basic tools: food, clothing, and shelter. We need to survive, and money also puts us in comfortable and happy environments. Poverty does not provide these survival tools, and it forces the impoverished into chronic stress mode. God blessed the rich with a choice; not so the poor. Think of Bill Gates, the billionaire. If he decided one day to join hands with the poor, he could do so quickly and easily. People would help him 24/7, even in the middle of a cold, stormy night.

On the other hand, if the poor made a decision to join hands with a billionaire, hundreds of years would pass, leaving only an empty grocery bag of hope at the end of the road—even on a beautiful, sunny day.

Before He created human beings, what was God doing? He must have been sitting idly on His throne doing nothing, with no one to contradict, guide, or punish, living in lonely confinement in an endlessly dull and boring life. It would be the same if all the citizens of Great Britain abandoned their respective regions, leaving the Royal Family all alone. Imagine how desperately lonely the monarchs would feel without the razzle-dazzle, pomp, and glory, and with no paparazzi to chase them around. Their Royal Highnesses would plead and beg their subjects to come back, starting with a hug and a kiss instead of a restrained handshake conducted with gloves up to the elbows.

At the start of Genesis, God longs for human partners as much as humans later long for Him. They are like any honeymoon couple, starting out full of promise and hope, only to experience sharp disappointments and display increasingly outrageous behavior, until they end up on the steps of divorce court, having clearly picked the wrong partners. The same holds true for God and His chosen people. In Deuteronomy 7:6, it is made clear to the Israelites that "You are a people holy to the Lord your God. The Lord your God has chosen you out of all the people of the earth to be His people, His treasured possession." But surely these are not the words of God. Why would God cherry-pick certain people out of so many other colors and tribes? Does God discriminate? Apparently He does, because He shows preference toward just a few of His supposedly equal human beings. It turns out to be such a bad choice, however, that He later abandons them. But you don't blame the horse if he loses the race; you blame the one who bet on the wrong horse.

Surah 31:31 asks, "See you not those ships sail through the oceans by the grace of God?" From the early days of sea passage to today, the ocean has remained a vast, unpredictable, and powerful place that wields a thousand challenges at once. Early mariners had such a daunting task that the Romans attributed the ocean's wild strength to the gods Poseidon and Neptune. Muslims did not name any sea gods, because there is no God but "Allah," who controls all. But Allah reminded mariners of the need for His grace and blessings when crossing those dominant and dangerous waters. The maritime industry changed dramatically between the times of Noah and Muhammad, and then it changed further to modern times. Tiny wooden boats became stable floating islands filled with all the comforts and luxuries of land. Mariners have accurate weather forecasts at their fingertips 24-7. Modern navigation equipment makes life on board safer and more luxurious. Hundreds of cruise ships move around the world every day, just for fun. In biblical times, sea passage was strictly a necessity—a means of acquiring food and conquering new lands. In the SOP (standard operating procedure) for modern sea travel, there's no mention of "sailing through the oceans by the grace of God." Old seafarers needed the grace of God for their safe return, but still many never made it back. Today, the grace of God has been replaced by the safe, strong, and stable architecture of human creation. Almighty God serves as the "captain" of blessings, grace, and sanctions to only a select few. But a human captain has a more noble code of conduct for all (women, children, and the elderly first, and the captain himself last) when the ship is going down.

If we look at the God of biblical times, He was active, alert, and ready for action, like an eager Boy Scout. He was involved in every detail of human life, rightly advising and guiding the Gang of Adam in the Garden of Eden. Unfortunately, that approach didn't work. Eve had a taste of forbidden fruit, and the result of her sin will be passed on to billions of future generations until Judgment Day. It is an absurd and senseless punishment from God. It would be the equivalent of punishing our kids and grandkids for crimes we committed. Judging from a few Bible verses, it sounds like the God of biblical times engaged strenuously with human beings. He taught, guided, and advised 24/7, like a kindergarten teacher.

When Moses came on the scene, however, God's level of involvement changed dramatically. He suddenly took a backseat and avoided the public eye. He admits this, saying, "And you shall see my back, but My face shall not be seen" (Exod. 33:23). He becomes quite selective about His company at this point, telling Moses in Exodus 34:3, "No one shall come up with you, Moses, and do not let anyone be seen on the mountain." God either developed stage fright or started having panic attacks over having brought humanity this far along. Finally, He stopped descending from His throne in Seventh Heaven, stopped taking strolls in the Garden of Eden, and stopped sending new messengers with reinvented holy books. God tried His best. He made agreements, distributed awards, and gave hope to humans. He punished them and even demolished the earth with floods in order to start over with a clean slate, with the next-most-righteous group of people. He sent the descendants of Abraham into slavery and then sent Moses to rescue them with the promise of a land of milk and honey. None of it worked.

Humanity's relationship with God has been a roller-coaster ride from the start—always a short-lived honeymoon followed by another and increasingly intense bout of wickedness in the world. Today, after a lot of hard work by God and His apostles for thousands of years, the followers of monotheistic religions comprise only around 50 percent of the world's population. This is not a passing grade. Even worse is the bitter irony that Jews, Christians, and Muslims, all followers of the same God, are ready to kill one another without considering their common God or seeking any consultation from Him. God adamantly picks and chooses His less-than-adequate holy messengers as He pleases, but He has not provided any recipe for brotherly love among various religions.

What God did provide were plenty of strict examples of what *not* to do, say, think, and eat, among other things. We get no such clear guidance on how to live peacefully with one another, but we do get a list of Do Nots. The Qur'an specifies what is forbidden (*haram*, in Arabic) in many verses. In Surah 2:173, humanity is enjoined not to eat pork: "He hath forbidden you dead meat, and blood, and the flesh of swine, and that on which any other name is invoked beside that of God." In Surah 5:3, God reveals a more specific list of Do Nots: "You are forbidden to eat carrion; blood; pig's meat; any animal over which any name other than God's has been invoked; any animal strangled or victim of a violent blow or a fall or gored or savaged by a beast of prey ... or anything sacrificed on idolatrous altars." The list of forbidden acts goes on to include "drawing marked arrows," which indicates divination, an old pagan practice. At least four other verses contain specific Do Nots, and in Surah 7:33, we come upon more spiritual concerns: "The things that my Lord indeed has forbidden (Haram) are: shameful deeds whether open or secret; sins and trespasses against truth or reason, assigning partners to God ..." Surah 6:151 includes this admonition: "What God hath forbade (Haram) from you, join not anything as equal with Him."

When it comes to human actions, the Qur'an discusses generic shameful deeds but gives no list of particular actions to avoid. What the Qur'an does make clear, however, through much repetition, is that assigning partners to God is the worst thing a person can do. It might have been more helpful if the Qur'an had spelled out other specific shameful deeds forbidden to humans. Surely we have the right to know what's right and wrong, lest we inadvertently violate behavioral code. Fear, punishment, hellfire, and heavenly rewards are mentioned in the Qur'an about 560 times—far more often than shameful deeds. It's like saying, "Speedy drivers will be fined," without specifying any speed limits. Before passing and enforcing a speeding law, authorities typically define an exact speed limit; that way, when they catch a speeder, they will know how harsh a penalty to impose.

Given such vague guidelines regarding behavior, it is easier for followers of faith to twist the words of any holy book to suit their own agenda, whatever that may be. It's not that difficult to claim that a certain verse from the Qur'an means what I say it means versus what the intention was at the time it was written—or even what the translation was intended to convey. People get away with labeling certain deeds shameful or sinful according to their needs. Most religions regard certain deeds as unacceptable, such as stealing, lying, cheating, killing, and bribing. But in reality, these immoral things occur whether the faithful Muslims show up to pray five times a day or not. Ironically, the most pious often make a great fuss over the proper enactment of prayers and the simplest of laws (e.g., not eating pork, not drinking or gambling), yet they freely and openly lie and cheat more than five times a day.

Returning to the issue of vague guidelines, none of holy books defines, specifically, who qualifies for access to heaven; they simply don't discuss the terms by which one can gain entry. Of course, the holy books do refer to sin many times, albeit vaguely, and they point out people who are "righteous," but there is no set of qualifiers that clearly delineates who "makes it" and who doesn't. So then, if someone—such as Abraham, David, and Moses—kills another human being, will he or she therefore be shut out of heaven? Can one murder be excused? What about two, three, or four? Or will it again be a matter of God's choice? All holy books repeat information regarding punishments, rewards, and Judgment Day, but never do they provide precise reasons that send a person to heaven or, conversely, to hell.

It's even more frustrating these days to try to determine where we'll end up in the afterlife, as moral laws have changed over time. Slavery is no longer allowed, divorce is a common practice, and for the most part, homosexuality is no longer openly condemned by the general public. Certain behaviors that were sins in biblical times have now become accepted. According to Romans 3:23, we are all sinners on one level: "For all have sinned, and come short of the glory of God." Psalm 58:3 relays this same sentiment: "The wicked are estranged from the womb: they go astray as soon as they be born, speaking lies." Presumably, this applies to popes, priests, apostles, saints, and ordinary folks alike, so one might assume that we're all in the running for heaven. But if God gives the green light to someone, will that person be cleansed somehow before entering heaven? Or will that person somehow pollute heaven, just as he or she did the earth? One of the frustrations that religion presents over and over again is a lack of clear direction. Much is left up to one's own imagination, opinion, or best guess.

More contradictions occur in the Qur'anic admonitions themselves. One admonition about wine and gambling, in particular, betrays inherent conflict. Surah 2:219 says, "In them is great sin and some 'profit' for men; but the sin is greater than the profit." If there's some good in drinking and gambling, and I'm a wine lover or a gambler, doesn't this scripture provide justification for me to keep on doing what I'm doing? Then again, we're told there is more sin than good involved in these actions—so what's a person to do? Despite the overall prohibition on drinking alcohol in the Qur'an, we come across some verses that seem to condone it—Surah 16:67, for example: "And from the fruits of the date-palm and vine, ye get out wholesome drink and food: behold, in this also is a sign for those who are wise." The Qur'an seems to allow alcohol in heaven, as well, as indicated in Surah 76:21: "And they will be adorned with bracelets of silver; and their Lord will give to them to drink of a wine, Sharab-e-Tahoora, pure and holy." If God offers you wine, it is pure and holy. If someone else offers you wine, however, it becomes sinful and disgusting.

Another conflict presented in the Qur'an is the parallel rejection and presence of poetry. Surah 26:224 equates poets as "those straying in evil." Despite this rejection of poetry as being tantamount to evil, no one can read the Qur'an without acknowledging that the language itself frequently approaches poetry. Surah 18:109 provides a good example of poetic language: "Say: 'If the oceans were ink to write out the words of my Lord, sooner would the ocean be exhausted than the words of my Lord, even if we added another ocean like it, for its aid.'" This surah is poetic enough to make the Qur'an the mother of all holy books. (Just to settle the matter, the Qur'an consists of 80,000 words, 6,200 verses, and 114 surahs. This amounts to fewer than 300 pages, which can easily be written with ink from a gallon-sized bucket. God can exhaust inks of oceans again and again, but He finished this book in only 80,000 words, leaving open many unexplained ideas that He presents in only two or three lines. He might have written more to provide clarification.)

A more interesting use of poetic language occurs in Surah 2:45: "Who is he that can loan to God a beautiful loan, which God will double to his credit and multiply many times? It's God that gives you want or plenty and to Him shall be your return." Yusuf Ali (Islamic scholar who translated Qur'an into English) asserts that "a beautiful loan" means "spending in the cause of God"—that is, giving to the poor or giving your time and energy to help build a mosque. Surah 57:18 explains that "those who give in charity" are lending God a beautiful loan, and "it shall increase manifold to their credit and they shall have a liberal reward." Yusuf Ali describes Qur'anic language as metaphorical in nature, especially regarding topics such as God's Kingdom, God's contribution, and the "secrets of the Unseen." We're still left, however, with the troubling notion of a loan, and these questions: "Why does God need a loan from a mere human?" and "Why would God need a human to get involved in His metaphorical credit and loan business?" The Holy Bank of God sounds like the Bank of Bernie Madoff and/

or many tricky Far East banks, which perpetrate crimes for their own profit with the false guarantee of doubling or otherwise multiplying a client's investment. Why does God sound like a modern salesperson, trying to take advantage of the weaknesses of the human brain in order to promote His domain? And if God will double and multiply credit, does this mean the donor will qualify to sit in the front row before the Lord in Seventh Heaven?

Excessive and potentially contradictory punishments also exist in the Qur'an. The punishment for stealing in Muhammad's day was to cut off the offender's hands (Surah 5:38). This sounds rather straightforward; you steal, you lose your hands. However, if Bernie Madoff steals $67 billion from his investors, and a twenty-year-old kid steals a 99-cent loaf of bread from a convenience store, do both thieves deserve to stand on the same platform of righteousness? We see more contradictory punishment in the Bible. In Matthew 18:8, we are told, "If your hand or foot causes you to stumble, cut it off and throw it away. It is better for you to enter life maimed or lame than to have two hands or two feet and to be thrown into eternal fire. And if your left eye causes you to stumble, tear it out and throw it away. Better for you to enter life with one eye than to have two eyes and to be thrown into the fire of Hell." If we followed the outdated laws in Matthew 18:8 and Surah 5:38, half the world would be limping and the other half blind. People would be hopping around on one leg, bumping into the one-eyed jacks. The only positive outcome of this punishment would be that one-handed humans would have fewer fingers with which to point at somebody else in blame!

Perhaps the most contradictory notion in the Qur'an is that of holy war. Everyone suffers tremendous losses in war, on every level—physical, financial, and emotional. According to some religions, however, wars fought in God's defense become "holy" wars, sanctified by God Himself. God, in turn, tries to make war's horrible endings palatable to human beings by promising them rewards. Surah 48:17 assures us that "he that obeys God and His apostles, God will admit him to Gardens beneath which rivers flow, and he who turns back, God will punish him with grievous penalty." Avoiding going to war in God's name constitutes a terrible insult to God and to fellow soldiers. In the Kingdom of God, fear, penalties, and rewards go hand in hand in exactly the same manner as in the kingdom of men. Most war propagandists convince common folk that if they don't take action now, they will be responsible for the kingdom's ruin. Sometimes no other plausible reason surfaces, and so, without providing a clear cause, the government trains the foot soldier to kill the enemy. After all the dust of war has settled and one side claims the title of victor, the award ceremonies begin. Anyone killed in a holy war receives the honored title of martyr and wins a front-row seat in God's Kingdom. The one who escapes death receives the title of *ghazi* ("warrior," in Arabic), and is given much fanfare for days. Today, we also honor our soldiers who return from war or die on the front lines; we present them with medals or give them a ceremonial burial with a 21-gun salute. Soon all is forgotten—until the new war starts with new excuses and new, fresh-faced soldiers.

# 7

## GOD'S WORK IS OFTEN SLOPPY, VAGUE, AND CHAOTIC

What religion allows people to do with the spoils of war may surprise you. The Bible allows the conquerors to take their pick of whatever they wish. Deuteronomy 21:10 states, "When you go to war against your enemies, the Lord hands them over to you and you take them captive. Suppose you see among captives a beautiful woman whom you wish and want to marry, so bring her to your home." Whether the woman wants marriage or not is irrelevant. What happened to God's motto of "fair and balanced" justice for the oppressed? It seems that all affairs of war, from beginning to end, reside in the tight fist of God. Oddly enough, although the conquered are good enough to steal from, they are not to be touched in times of peace. It's okay to take your enemy's women during battle, but don't touch them otherwise, because they don't live up to your standards of hygiene. Surah 9:28 declares, "O ye who believe! Truly the Pagans are unclean; so let them not, after this year of theirs, approach the sacred mosque." According to Yusuf Ali, "unclean" is both a literal and a metaphorical reference.[44] Islam contains strict rules regarding physical cleanliness, equating a clean body with a pure mind and heart; non-Muslims are automatically suspect in terms of hygiene. In the early days, it was easy to label pagan rivals as unclean, factually and metaphorically; it was an easy way to deny them access to the sacred mosque. Pagans and monotheists, however, were actually in the same boat when it came

---

[44] *Holy Qur'an*, 446.

to hygiene; access to means of physical cleanliness was exactly the same for both parties.

The world comprises 50 percent "pagans" (nonbelievers and polytheists) and 50 percent monotheists. Now, let's take the example of two countries: India, whose people typically follow the polytheistic Hindu faith, and its neighboring country Pakistan, which has a majority of Muslims, monotheists. They live grudgingly side by side with exactly the same standards of physical cleanliness and purity of mind and heart. Surah 9:28's guidelines for the approach by pagans, Hindus, and Buddhists to the sacred mosque are discriminatory and biased. Pagans deserve the same right as anyone else to enter the sacred mosque. The doors should be open to all people, believers and nonbelievers. After all, you don't promote your religion with the front door locked and someone checking IDs.

Apart from religious rituals, standards of physical hygiene typically depend on environmental resources. In wealthy, industrialized nations, it is relatively easy to maintain cleanliness due to the availability of running water. In the poorest nations, regardless of people's beliefs, maintaining cleanliness can turn into a challenge. As for purity of mind and heart, they are not necessary reflected in physical cleanliness. How many dirty atheists do we see roaming the streets, robbing and killing people? Actually, the supposedly "clean" in both the physical and social senses are the ones that pose a greater threat to society today (e.g., pedophile priests and criminal politicians).

As we have seen so far, religion flourishes on miracles, mysteries, prophesies, and poetic language. It is also full of unfulfilled promises and ongoing misinterpretations and contradictions. Perhaps the greatest religious misinterpretation and contradiction of all times involves "Jesus, the Son of God." Through the angel Gabriel, God informed "the Virgin Mary" that she would bear a son who would be the savior of the world. However, the Hebrew word for Mary, *Almah*, merely denotes a "young woman" and not necessarily a virgin. What proof did these Gospel writers have that Jesus was born from a virgin named Mary? How could they have kept track of a woman's virginity? Even if "Luke" and "Matthew" had had a chance to study Joseph and Mary's intimate life

24/7 with a magnifying glass, claiming that she was a virgin is as absurd as me telling my neighbors that the tree in my backyard bears hundred-dollar bills whenever a stock market crash occurs. Why did God have to make Jesus born of a virgin? It should be enough that in Genesis 1:28, God blesses Adam and Eve and says, "Be fruitful and multiply, fill the earth and subdue it." The writers of the Gospels of Luke and Matthew use the word *virgin* for their own purposes: if Mary (a.k.a. Almah) was a virgin, then the birth of Jesus is far more likely to have been divine or miraculous in origin. It appears as though the task of the Gospels of Luke and Matthew is to put Jesus in the same category as God—which, of course, is the whole crux of Christianity (Jesus = God).

Also, by the time writers began creating the Gospels, they were well aware of the social stigma against unwed mothers. It was important to them to have Mary appear as virtuous as possible—hence the claim of her virginity. Otherwise, Mary would have been subject to punishment under the law, and the Mother of God cannot have a criminal record! Injunctions against fornication exist in both the Bible and the Qur'an. Surah 24:1 specifies punishment for fornication: "The woman and man guilty of adultery or fornication … Flog each of them with a hundred stripes." Interestingly, the punishment is not as specific for two men engaging in the same crimes, as Surah 4:16 acknowledges: "If two men among you are guilty of lewdness, punish them both. If they repent and amend, leave them alone." No comment by Yusuf Ali explains this difference.

The constant backdrop to all sins mentioned in the Qur'an is the understanding that God is omniscient: "With Him are the keys of the unseen … Not a leaf does fall but with His knowledge" (6:59). References to God's superhuman qualities, character, and power appear at least eight hundred times in the Qur'an; He is a being of boundless virtues and infinite knowledge, organizing the entire universe with the utmost precision. The question remains: Why, then, is His work so often sloppy and chaotic? Floods, droughts, wildfires, and human-made disasters are prime examples of God's undisciplined and untidy world. Whenever I set the timer on my microwave, garden sprinkler, or oven, they stop precisely when they're supposed to. God doesn't seem to have a good working clock; it just keeps ticking, causing floods, hurricanes, and all sorts of other disasters. Hundreds of thousands of innocent people, many of them staunch believers in God, lose their lives every year. We are not in the Old Testament times, when God often destroyed generations due to human wickedness. The generations of Thamud, Ad, Madyan, and Noah were all eliminated due to defiance of God's signs and prophets. Still, that is not a proper or logical reason to kill someone. As Surah 2:256 of the Qur'an reminds us, "Let there be no compulsion in religion." People have always had the ability to choose good or evil, whether or not they believe in God and His apostles, signs, and holy books.

We have seen many aspects of God so far—God the Creator, God the Magician, God the Too Human, God the Inept, and even God the Punisher/Destroyer. There are many biblical and Qur'anic verses that depict God killing people for no obvious reason. On average, today's common folk appear much less defiant than those of previous generations; many people accept heavenly signs and holy books sent hundreds and hundreds of years ago. Half the world attends places of worship, praises God, and even continues to make sacrifices to God, and He continues to allow believers and nonbelievers alike to be killed to this very day. This disturbing fact raises questions about the destruction of past generations or even more recent ones. Was it just the luck of the draw that so many people were trapped in the net of Hurricane Katrina? Nearly two thousand innocent believers and nonbelievers lost their lives. They were not handpicked for destruction like the wickedly defiant generations of Noah, Thamud, Ad, and Madyan.

Google the word *covenant* and you will find that it is "a written agreement or promise under seal between two parties." The common understanding of the word *witness* is one who sees, hears, or knows by his or her personal presence—a bystander. Qur'an 3:81 states, "Behold! God took the covenant of the prophets, saying: 'I give you a book and wisdom; then comes to you an Apostle, confirming what is with you; do you believe in him and render him help.' God said: 'Do you agree and take this My covenant as binding on you?' They said: 'We agree.' He said, 'Then bear witness, and I am with you among the witnesses.'" But what procedure did God follow when making this covenant with the people?

Mostly, we hear only that a covenant has been made, but not how. Surah 3:187 states, "And remember God took a covenant from the People of the Book, to make it known and clear to mankind … but they threw it away behind their backs." (People of the Book refers to followers of Monotheistic Abrahamic religions. This includes all Christians and all children of Israel.)

How did this agreement between God and the People of the Book take place? Were the People of the Book present at a certain location for this covenant, or did the tribal chief talk to God, as usual, and then relay the message? Did some holy man later "share" God's message with the people under threat of Judgment Day? How were the two parties in the contract represented? How many people approved this binding agreement? It is no wonder that, after a while, the People of the Book "threw away the books and covenant behind their backs" and moved on with life.

Rainbows became another questionable vehicle by which God makes covenants with people. Genesis 9:13 uses God's words: "I have set my bow in the clouds, and it shall be the sign of covenant between Me and earth." The next verse states, "When I bring clouds over the earth and the bow is seen over the clouds, I will remember my covenant between Me and you and every living creature of all flesh. The waters shall never again become a flood to destroy all flesh." Older myths and legends from other religions feature the sun, moon, and stars as the gods and children of gods; they frequently appear behind the hideouts of lightning, thunder, clouds, and rainbows. The supreme, monotheistic God eliminated the sun, moon, and star gods, but it was hard for Him to break ties with the lightning, thunder, clouds, and rainbows. He essentially kept Himself intact in the sky. People in Noah's and Abraham's times had no understanding of the science behind clouds, rainbows, earthquakes, and thunder. They automatically attributed these phenomena to the existence of a supreme power that controlled all natural forces.

Dazzling and mysterious to people of ancient times, the rainbow came to be considered miraculous; it appears in every culture and religion in the world. Greco-Roman mythology, the Hindu religion, Chinese mythology, and Armenian mythology—and let's not forget the Irish leprechaun with his pot of gold—all include rainbow myths. In the Sumerian "Epic of Gilgamesh," a rainbow is the "jeweled necklace of the great mother Ishtar."[45] In Incan mythology, God put a rainbow in the sky as a sign of His promise that He would never destroy the earth with a flood.[46]

Let's look at the simple formation of clouds and rainbows. Clouds and rainbows have no traces of God floating in them that scientists have ever found. Clouds are a visible mass of water droplets or ice crystals suspended in the atmosphere. If air cools to its dew point and becomes soaked, it normally sheds the vapor that it can no longer hold, which condenses into clouds. A rainbow is the result of optical and meteorological causes. When the sun shines on droplets of moisture in the earth's atmosphere, a multicolored arc appears in the sky on the opposite side of the sun. That's the simple explanation. So how does a rainbow become a contract between humanity and God? If God places a contract in the sky, how can human beings see what's in it? A covenant with God would be as hard to find as an Irish leprechaun with his pot of gold.

Furthermore, writers of the holy books took advantage of humans' propensity to believe in miracles, mysteries, legends, and myths, without giving any genuine reason or proof for the existence of God. First, they have God pick a holy prophet of His choosing, as Surah 3:179 confirms: "But He chooses of His apostles whom He pleases." Next, God makes a covenant with this holy prophet and gives him a book of rules. He's like a dictator who picks a favored lieutenant who then forces the dictator's rules down the throat of an entire nation. No wonder people so often rejected God's clear signs and messages; they were "given" them under duress.

Generally speaking, a covenant is an agreement between two parties that is witnessed, signed, dated, testified to, and kept in a safe place. It describes tasks, duties, and time frames, and it provides information on what recourse to follow if disagreement or default occurs between the two parties. A religious covenant is a contract made by God with a

---

[45] "Rainbows in Culture," *Wikipedia*, last modified August 10, 2014, http://en.wikipedia.org/wiki/Rainbows_in_culture.

[46] "Flood Myth," *Wikipedia*, last modified October 7, 2014, http://en.wikipedia.org/wiki/Flood_myth.

religious community or humanity. In Genesis 9:12, for example, God says, "Never again shall I send a flood to destroy the earth. I have set My bow in the clouds as a sign of the contract between Me and earth." Well, we all know that God sends floods every year on a regular basis. Highly destructive floods ruin the terrain, obliterate animal and human habitats, and kill people for no reason. So how do we hold God accountable for this breach of contract? Once we find God's sign of a rainbow in the sky, do we yell, scream, and throw stones in the air to get His attention? Again, holy messengers created these elaborate religious metaphors to keep a firm grip on the minds of innocent humans.

For God, the worst sin against Him is rejection. In this way, He is much like an earthly king who claims treason when he encounters resistance or potential rivals. Humans may get away with crimes against one another, but if they harm a king in any way, they're playing with their lives. The Qur'an mentions the sin of rejecting God or equating Him with others more than 290 times. Surah 4:48 states, "God forgives not that partners should be set up with Him. He forgives anything else, to whom He pleases, but to set up a partner with God is to devise a sin most wicked indeed." We see this same theme in Surah 4:116: "God forgets not the sin of joining other gods with Him. He forgives whom He pleases other sins than this: one, who joins other gods with God, hath strayed far, far away from the right." Even more emphatically, we are told in Surah 8:55 that "the worst of the beasts in the sight of God are those who reject Him: they will not believe." One example of punishment for this sin appears in Surah 8:54: "They treated as false the signs of their Lord: so we destroyed them for their crimes, and we drowned the people of Pharaoh: for they were all oppressors and Evildoers."

# 8

## GOD PATS HIS OWN BACK, DESPITE A FAILING GRADE

Human beings also hate rejection and love to punish those who disagree with them. Looking back through human history, we can see many examples of men who defied a king, the vast majority of whom ended up on the chopping block. Humans often lack judgment, putting their emotions at the forefront to fulfill their dominant desires. So does God, as noted in the surah at the end of the last chapter; He simply drowned the people of Pharaoh in a flash. This horrible act speaks to God's likeness to humans—which, again, suggests that the holy books are the products of human brains.

In keeping with God's extreme dislike for rejection, He insists on being first and being humanity's sole focus. Qur'an 22:18 alludes to punishment for disregarding God in any way: "To God bow down in worship all things that are in Heaven and on earth, sun, moon, stars, hills, trees, animals, and a great number among human beings. But a great number are fit for punishment ..." Also, that passage assumes that all things in heaven and on earth are aware of God's requirement to be worshipped and put above all things. In biblical times there was no census. The writers of the holy books could only surmise that whatever message a prophet preached to his community would spread out in a radius of a few hundred miles. They had no idea that people existed in faraway places such as Australia or Russia, as we call them today. And so Surah 3:83, which states, "All creatures in the Heavens and on earth have, willingly or unwillingly, bowed to His will," makes an assumption that reflects the time in which the Qur'an was written, and not fact. Then just a few verses later, Surah 3:86 asks, "How shall God guide those who reject faith after they accepted it and bore witness the Apostle was true?" These surahs seem to contradict each other. In Surah 3:83, all creatures in heaven and earth have bowed to His will (that is, accepted Islam). Yet Surah 3:86 calls into question the very statements made in 3:83. It stands to reason that if all creatures of heaven and earth bowed to God's will, then no rejecters of Islam would exist. Surah 3:86 almost seems to question whether God can actually do anything about the ones who reject Him. Rejecting Him sounds like a shock to God. If any creature rejected God's message, it was more than likely because the message was not appealing or useful at the time. Perhaps the holy messengers themselves were not appealing; none of the 124,000 managed to persuade a simple but emphatic message: "Bow to the will of God."

Let's take another look at Surah 22:18 and analyze the verse—not metaphorically, but literally, based on facts and numbers. The surah states, "To God bow down in worship all things that are in Heaven and on earth, sun, moon, stars, hills, trees, animals; and a great number among Mankind? But a great number (also) such as are fit for punishment ..." All creatures of heaven and earth comprise billions; it is a big number. First, we can narrow it down to the creatures of the earth, with which we are moderately familiar. Next, we can narrow it down further, to humans only. The Qur'an contains many verses that say bowing to God's will means accepting Islam, but that's not so for the Old or New Testaments. There is no biblical equalizer to Surah 3:83 that says to bow to God's will is to accept Judaism or Christianity.

Saying that bowing to God's will means accepting Islam, then, is as factual as claiming that God is a Republican, Santa is a Democrat, and Satan is an Independent. So what happened in that vast span of two thousand five hundred years between Abraham and Muhammad? During that time, three major religions unfailingly revolved around one another in a 1.25-million-square-mile area in the Middle East. That's only 2.1 percent of the earth's surface area. Holy messengers talked and shouted to the masses, struggling and sweating and often subjecting themselves to unbearable circumstances, all to deliver a message. They traveled all around their little patch of land, and some even "traveled" to heaven itself, but unfortunately, they all missed 97.9 percent of the land where they could have delivered God's message. The historic record suggests that Muhammad was the one who started Islam. Muslims, who now represent 20 percent of the world's population, willingly or unwillingly "bow to the will of God." That is a poor percentage for Allah. According to a recent survey, the world's population now stands at 7.185 billion.[47] Out of this total number, religious populations are represented as follows:[48]

Christians: 30% (2 Billion)
Buddhists: 29% (1.9 Billion)
Muslims: 20% (1.57 Billion)
Nonreligious: 16% (1.1 Billion)
Hindus: 14% (1 Billion)
Jews: 0.19% (13 Million)

About half of all people in the world, then, are monotheistic believers (Jews, Christians, and Muslims, for a total of 50.19 percent). The rest (Buddhists, Hindus, atheists, and agnostics) make up the remaining 49.81 percent. Every holy messenger, from Abraham to Muhammad, struggled and fought to convince people to accept his message from God. Presumably, omniscient God, exhausted with having to work so hard to win only 50 percent of the population, gave up His plan. A final point: although an exact count of individual world religions is impossible to know, a recent estimate is around forty-two hundred.[49] One can't help but ask: if there is only one God, or even if there are several gods, why are there thousands of religions? Humans continue to invent new religions and beliefs.

[47] "World Population," *Wikipedia*, last modified October 4, 2014, http://en.wikipedia.org/wiki/World_population.
[48] "List of Religious Populations," Wikipedia, last modified September 30, 2014, http://en.wikipedia.org/wiki/List_of_religious_populations.
[49] Robert Pollock, *World Religions, Beliefs and Traditions from Around the World* (Fall River Press, 2008).

# 9

## ANGELS

Having examined earth's religious composition, let's now consider a few identifiable heavenly creatures revealed so often in holy books. Angels feature most prominently and seem always on the go. In early scriptures they're seen walking around in the wilderness, giving blessings, glad tidings, warnings, and commands. Although angels typically served as God's messengers and played an important role in God's communication with humanity early on, He gradually reduced their appearances on earth. Following Muhammad's long stint as the "last messenger" and the writing of the Qur'an, angels started to vanish. Did God give up on the idea of a new holy messenger, or did He run out of messages because they had no effect on humans? Did God surrender to the will of genius, the self-sufficient new breed of twenty-first-century "gods" (the technical gurus of today)? Perhaps God is considering investing in real estate somewhere other than earth. Like humans, He may have become bored with angels, religion, the earth, or even humans themselves.

It's quite possible that God started to give up shortly after sending His only son to represent Him on earth. This is hard to imagine, but then we've already seen that God lacks several key coping skills, and that His parental skills as Heavenly Father are woefully lacking. In this case, looking at the various birth stories of Jesus, we see angels in action in each one. Let's look at the birth story as presented in Qur'an 19:17 and 19–21: "We placed a screen to screen herself from them. Then We sent to her an angel and he appeared before her as a man in all respects ...

He said, 'I am only a messenger from my Lord to announce to the gift of a holy son.' 'How shall I have a son, since no man has touched me and I am not unchaste?' He said: 'So it will be: Thy Lord said, that is easy for Me, and We wish to appoint him as a sign to men and a mercy from Us.'" At this point, we need to put Mary in the context of a regular family. A so-called angel appeared as a man to a young girl in the middle of the night, placed a screen between them—presumably for modesty's sake—and claimed to give a gift of a holy son. First, how inappropriate is this? Screen or no screen, you don't drop in on a lady unannounced in the middle of the night—and certainly not in biblical times. This would have offended anyone's sensibilities. A woman could not simply hang out with a man in the middle of the night, talking, no matter how innocent or important the subject matter. Second, Mary did not ask for any proof of identity or clarification from the so-called angel, who appeared to be a man in all respects. She took his word on such an important physical and divine issue based on a few words, and she did this without consulting her betrothed, Joseph, or some other holy chiefs of the tribe. The whole story, told in only four verses, seems sketchy, and the angel appears as a somewhat shady character. If we fathers and husbands of the world, past and present, considered the story in the context of our own daughters and wives, I am sure we would have lots of pressing questions.

It is possible that the angel was, in fact, a real man named Panthera, a Roman soldier, as described by some academics.[50] Both the Jewish Talmud (the Old Testament) and the work of the Philosopher Celsus,[51] a second-century writer, contain rumors of a Roman soldier named Pondera or Panthera that suggest he may have been the one to visit Mary and announce her pregnancy. If that's true, it's no wonder Mary isolated herself to give birth to Jesus; she wished to avoid humiliation in her community. That practice still takes place today in certain parts of society: families let their unwed daughters leave home during pregnancy to avoid embarrassment.

---

[50] James D. Tabor, *The Jesus Dynasty* (Simon & Schuster, 2006), 65.
[51] "Celsus," *Wikipedia*, last modified September 13, 2014, http://en.wikipedia.org/wiki/Celsus.

In sharp contrast to Mary's angel, Hagar's angel takes a much more aggressive and conniving stance. In Genesis 16:8, Hagar tells her angel, "I am running away from my mistress Sarai." Given this information, we might expect an angel to take a compassionate interest in Hagar's situation. Hagar must be pretty desperate, escaping alone into the wilderness with no shelter and no food. Angels are supposed to be gentle guardians and the bearers of glad tidings, right? We expect them to be kind and benign, as they typically appear on TV. Not this one. In Genesis 16:9–11, Hagar's angel responds tersely: "Return to your mistress and agree to her. Now you have conceived. You shall bear a son. Call him Ishmael." Pretty direct and forceful words. This angel of the Lord orders Hagar to return to her mistress against her wishes. Next, the angel puts the icing on this bitter cake by forcing submission on Hagar, ordering her pregnancy out of the blue and against her wishes. So now Hagar has to go back to a tyrant, carrying an unwanted child and overseen by an angel that acts more like a member of the Mafia. He even names the future child for her. Not a good situation. Hagar does return to her Mistress Sarah and Master Abraham, but only to endure further fights and humiliation. From that point on, holy scriptures vary on this story.

# 10

## GOD AND HIS PROPHET'S
## METHOD OF DELIVERY

Surah 42:51 states, "It is not fitting for a man that God speak to him, except by inspiration or from behind veil, or by sending messenger ..." The term *inspiration* is generally interpreted as an idea God has infused into the human heart or mind. God's language of inspiration, however, is hard for an ordinary human to understand, so it is not reliable. For humans to be convinced of an idea and to take a proposed action, they need to be able to grasp the reason for the action and the evidence that supports taking the action. They also need to see the potential results of taking such an action. It's the same simple strategy behind buying a car. First, the buyer needs a reason to choose a particular car out of many. Second, evidence must exist as to the car's durability and performance relative to its price. Third, the seller must impress the buyer with a solid sales presentation. Similarly, when considering electing a person to a position of leadership, the voter needs to be convinced by the leader's persuasive powers, speaking skills, intelligence, knowledge, and experience. In other words, the voter needs to approve of the candidate's resume. Most important, the candidate must be able to convince people to vote for him or her in particular. There must be clear and convincing reasons to believe that the candidate means what he or she says and will be the best person to represent important matters to the higher leadership.

God's method of delivery has worked as inefficiently as the US Postal

Service. His delivery is slow, and every year He demands more for His service. Throughout history, God has sent divine messages through 124,000 special message carriers—all of whom were consistently challenged, confronted, and heckled, the way mail carriers are pursued by dogs. Rather than learning from His mistakes or giving up on His mission, God simply kept cranking out the same service, delivering messages through ineffective people or through imposed disasters, but always indirectly. Messages delivered from behind veils rarely work for humans. We wouldn't vote for a candidate on earth who speaks through a veil. We are less likely to accept a divine message this way. God pushed hard for thousands of years, putting His holy messengers on the front lines. Many gave their lives in the line of duty to fulfill God's commands. So why did God always stay behind a veil? Is He too shy to face human beings on earth? Is He perhaps too comfortable in Seventh Heaven? If God decided to face us directly one day, what results might this meeting have? If I were a gambler, I would bet nothing, because sooner or later we are going to meet God anyway, according to Surah 3:143: "And now you have seen Him with your own eyes." This verse refers to life after death.

One holy messenger, Jesus, reached mythic proportions that continue to this day. Written largely by unknown writers, the Gospel stories promote a certain image of Jesus for a particular audience. About thirty years after Jesus's death, his story was first told by the writer(s) of Mark, followed by "Matthew" and "Luke." These first three Gospels are called "synoptic," as the stories are similar. The writers' job was somewhat like an advertiser's; they aimed to garner a following for Jesus in order to promote Christianity. Their audience included everyone who had heard of Jesus as well as those who were not aware of Jesus's teachings. What the writers omitted from the Gospels is just as interesting as what they included. Clearly, they show Jesus in the best light, as a kind and patient but passionate and strong person with God-given special powers. They leave out a huge section of Jesus's early life, however. Each Gospel story skips Jesus's formative childhood years, stopping at infancy and then jumping to his adult ministry. Readers can only speculate about the reason for this glaring absence. Perhaps the information was just lacking or not noteworthy. Perhaps the writers' assumption was that Jesus was doing what any good Jewish boy did in his day, going to temple and learning his religion. Or maybe there were other reasons we'll never know. In any case, the reader can't help but feel cheated and is left to ask, "What really went on in this missing time frame?"

Of all the holy messengers, Jesus seems to be the most realistic and honest about who he was. He has no illusions of grandeur, like his predecessors Moses or even Abraham. In Mark 8: 27–28, Jesus is on his way to Caesarea and asks his disciples, "'Who do people say that I am?' They answered him, 'John the Baptist,' and others 'Elijah,' and others, 'One of the prophets.'" Interestingly, Jesus warns them not to tell others he is the messiah. So why would Jesus ask, "Who do people say that I am?" Either he had no confidence, or he had doubts himself about being the messiah. The answer from his followers confirms that. Also, why would his people identify him with John the Baptist, Elijah, or one of the other prophets? Then Jesus puts this question to his disciples: "But who do you say that I am?" By now, Jesus, the Son of God, should know where he stands with his disciples and what they think of him. By asking ambiguous questions, Jesus proves that he is not a leader, a messiah, or the Son of God. The third question we have to ask is why Jesus forbade the disciples to tell others that he was the messiah. Being a humble and honest man, Jesus told the truth. Jesus did not like the idea of being labeled what he was not.

Christian Gospels and Muslim Hadiths have many similarities. The Gospels tell the story of Jesus's birth, ministry, and death and include what are believed to be his direct statements. Hadiths provide a written narration of many events in the lives of Muhammad and his followers. They also include direct statements and sayings that Muhammad shared throughout his life with various people, mostly his companions. The Hadiths were passed orally from one generation to the next until several narrators recorded them in writing. They form an essential part of the Islamic faith and are thought to provide adjunct teachings to the Qur'an. (For a book that claims to have answers for every present worldly problem and the spiritual answers regarding life after death, the Qur'an apparently leaves many questions unanswered.) Many Muslims rely on the Hadiths to amplify their understanding of the Qur'an and fill in the gaps. The reliability of the Hadiths' narrators is therefore crucial. Just as with the Qur'an, however, questions arise regarding the possible hidden agendas of each narrator in recording the Hadiths. Certain narrators followed Abu-Bakr, others followed Umar, and still others relied on Ali ibn Abu Talib. Abu-Bakr, Umar, Uthman, and Ali were the first four caliph of Islam. Ironically, differences among narrators may very well impact how the narrations were passed down, leaving Muslims to ask, "How do we verify the original text?"

Although all monotheists share the same God, they cause great unrest and sometimes violence when they replace God's words with their own, passing their ideas off as God's truth. This unfortunate practice causes many divisions within and between faiths. The first monotheistic religion, Judaism, has four main historical divisions: Sadducees, Pharisees, Essenes, and Zealots. The modern Jewish movements cover; Orthodox, Reform, Conservative, Hasidism, and Kabbalah. Christianity encompasses a wide range of distinct denominations, including Catholics, Protestants, Methodists, Lutherans, Baptists, Mormons, Presbyterians, evangelists, and many others. Islam has various sects, also, such as Sunnis, Shi'ites, Sufis, and Qadiani, to name a few. Despite the commonalities among most religions, people of faith tend to highlight and focus on the differences. We have only to look at the state of present-day Iraq to see how sectarianism ruins human relations and affects the rest of the world. Natural compassion and other noble human qualities seem to vanish in the face of religious territorialism. Each party insists on being right without hearing a word the other parties have to say. They all miss the glaring fact that they're guilty of the same thing! It seems that religion brings out the worst in people. Nonbelievers may just be the most righteous group, oddly enough; with no stake in any particular doctrine, they shake their heads in wonder from the sidelines. After all, nonbelievers are not the ones running around Iraq and other parts of the world with guns blazing.

Having just discussed some of humanity's worst qualities, let's return to the Garden of Eden for a moment. In the first crime of the universe, Adam points a finger at Eve, who points a finger at the serpent, poor creature of God. The serpent can't point a finger at anyone. Genesis 3:14 informs us of the degrading manner in which God makes the serpent leave the garden: "On your belly you shall go, and dust you shall eat all the days of your life." Then the second crime of humanity occurs. In Genesis 4:8, Cain murders his brother Abel. In simple mathematical terms, now 25 percent of the earth's population is gone. Genesis 4:3 tells us that "during time, Cain brought to the Lord an offering of the fruit and Abel brought the first production of his flock." The Lord accepted Abel's offerings but not Cain's. That made Cain angry. Omniscient God adds fuel to the fire by asking Cain, "Why you are angry?"

Now let us put this in simple human terms. Think of any family today, anywhere on earth. Two young kids bring baked goods they made from scratch, on their own, to your house. One baked cupcakes, the other cookies. The cupcakes taste wonderful, but the cookies, unfortunately, lack sugar. Wouldn't you welcome both children with open arms anyway? You wouldn't want one child to feel bad. Rather than reject the cookies, you might ask the child how much sugar he put in the cookies and suggest that he put more in next time. You certainly wouldn't reject him. God's negative reaction fueled Cain's jealousy, which turned into murderous rage against Abel. God sets up favorite people and groups of people, causing mayhem among everyone else. As we have seen, He even favors those who fight for Him over those who don't, as Surah 4:95 reveals: "God granted a grade higher, who strive and fight with their goods and persons than to those who sit at home ..." Yusuf Ali explains the verse this way: "There are degrees among men and women of faith. There are people with natural inertia; they do the minimum required of them, but no more. But those strong in will, determined to conquer every obstacle ... In times of 'Jihad' people give their all, even their lives, for a common cause. They must be accounted more gloriously than those who sit at home."[52] Surah 4:95 serves as yet another example of how God thinks with a human brain and human logic. When we recruit a soldier to fight in war, we admire him and call him a patriot. On the other hand, the young man flying anti-war flags that read "Make Love Not War"

---

[52] *Holy Qur'an*, 211.

never gets any admiration. Rather, he is seen as an outcast. In Surah 4:95, God pushes hard to promote the agenda of war, with the same logic and reasoning as a human; after all, the writers (or compilers) of the Qur'an were human beings.

Before the arrival of Islam, human civilizations embraced and moved through many beliefs, religions, and cultures within a few thousand years. Surah 5:3 states, "This day have I perfected your religion for you and chosen Islam as your religion." Did Christianity and Judaism serve just as testing grounds, then, for God to root out faults and perform experiments? The Old and New Testaments must have included some margin of error for God to replace them with the Qur'an. After the roller-coaster ride of earlier generations, did God finally fine-tune Judaism and Christianity to create Islam as the perfect religion? It certainly looks that way. If that's true, then why did it take God a few thousand years to think up, plan, and complete the "perfect" religion of Islam, which clearly has its own pitfalls? If He is omniscient, why didn't God know to introduce Islam from the very beginning? And, again, why not just use the magical word *Be* to create Islam? (Surah 2:117: "When He decreed a matter, He said: 'Be' and it was.") God created earth, heaven, the universe, and even Jesus with the word *Be*, but creating the perfect ideology took omniscient God a few thousand years. The irony remains, of course, that the world of seven billion people is in as much chaos today as it was when there were only four people alive: Adam, Eve, Abel, and Cain.

We see another example of God's puzzling lack of omniscience in Surah 5:109: "One day will God gather the Apostles together, and ask: 'What was the response you received from men to your teaching?' They will say 'We have no knowledge: It's you who know in full all that is hidden.'" God has no need to ask such an absurd question from His apostles. Why should He ask anything if He knows all the answers? Both the question and answer seem irrational and improper. God already knows the details of all their hardships—even the crucifixion Jesus endured. The apostles' reply, "We don't know," is like a young kid's reply; parents hear this kind of thing all the time. These apostles clearly don't qualify for the job assigned to them. If they cannot give a truthful answer to a simple question from their boss (God), then they are not intelligent enough to perform their job. After He hears His apostles' response, what God says has no bearing on the question. He asks a question and, as usual, starts out with self-praise, reminding His disciples that He holds the power ("and Jesus made a bird from clay with my Leave"). Instead of offering self-praise, God should give his apostles a bit of guidance so they can come up with a better answer next time.

Let's put this scenario in the context of corporate America, with the chief executive officer of a bank in the role of God. The CEO calls a meeting with senior management and explains his new policies to pass on to their staff. A year later, the CEO asks the same question of senior management that God asked of His apostles: "What response did you get to your teaching?" The last thing the CEO would like to hear is "We don't know, but you should." Instead of going into details and giving better guidelines, the CEO immediately starts blowing his horn, just like God. He should offer solutions to problems instead. If I were a member of the bank's board of directors, I would recommend the CEO's removal and examine the competence of senior management! It was poor form for God to ask a question and then answer it Himself, assuming the apostles' response. It's the same as a teacher who asks students a question and then answers it himself before they can respond, as if to say, "I know what you're going to say, so here's the answer." The holy messengers' response suggests that they are either lying or trying to be diplomatic—or perhaps that they really don't know the answer. The same was true for the people exposed to the holy messengers' teachings; they often just didn't know how to reply to new management—or they flat-out rejected it, as the following verses from the Qur'an clearly show, starting with Abraham:

+ 29:24: "So naught was the answer of Abraham's people except they said: 'Slay him or burn him.'"
+ 2:90–91: "In that they deny the revelation which God has sent down ... they say, 'We believe in what was sent down to us': Yet

they reject all besides, even it be truth confirming what is with them ..."

+ 7:75–76: "Know you indeed that Salih is an Apostle from his Lord ... The arrogant party said: 'For our part, we reject what you believe in.'"

Regarding Abraham, to this day he holds a high position of respect and admiration as the forefather of three major world religions. Abraham appeared more adept than Moses and even Noah in handling the masses. He had a more defined and advanced sense of managerial leadership. He was a fast mover and talker, always quick to justify his words and actions by citing revelations and God's will. His assertions that "God said so" and "God sent me a vision" staved off many controversies that otherwise could have caused a great deal of trouble for Abraham and all God's messengers. We see this dynamic at work in the following verses:

+ "Abraham rose by night and burned all in flames and his brother Haran in-house of Idols" (Book of Jubilees, 12:12–14). (According to Abraham, God prompted these actions.)
+ "Now the Lord said to Abraham, 'Go from your country ...'" (Gen. 12:1).
+ "After these things the word of Lord came to Abraham in a vision ..." (Gen. 15:1).
+ "When Abraham was 99 years old, the Lord appeared to Abraham ..." (Gen. 17).
+ "The Lord appeared to Abraham by the oaks of Mamre ... a son promised to Abraham and Sarah" (Gen. 18).
+ "The Lord said to Abraham, 'Take your son Isaac, and offer him there as burnt offering ...'" (Gen. 22).

Abraham burned his brother Haran to death and nearly killed his son Isaac to appease God. It appears that Abraham played the role of the radical in his public life, but in private, he seems more of a pushover. In Genesis 16:2, "Sarah said to Abraham, 'Go into my slave girl; it may be that I shall gain children by her.'" Sarah has given up hope of having her own children, and so she orders Abraham to have a child for her with her slave girl, Hagar. Abraham complies submissively with Sarah's demand, without using his judgment. In Abraham's family, Sarah wears the pants and carried a whip. She is a selfish, opportunistic, and pushy housewife. So Abraham has relations with Hagar, who conceives a child, Ishmael. Later, in Genesis 2:10, Sarah says to Abraham, "cast out this slave woman with her son." Again, Abraham follows her orders, sacking Hagar and their son. What human deprives his young son of food and shelter? It is ironic that Abraham, portrayed as a friend of God, can't see after the welfare of his son and Hagar.

Where is the morality among these holy figures? Sarah commands her husband to "go into" Hagar, a slave. Of course, slavery was accepted in those days, and the phrase "go into" was a normal biblical euphemism for sexual activity. But didn't Sarah and Abraham have the decency to think through what might become of a child born out of wedlock and out of desperation? What happened to the rite of holy matrimony? How does Abraham even qualify to be a father? How do any of the holy messengers qualify to lead others in terms of morality? Rachel and Leah continue the same trend of immorality. Genesis 30:9 tells us that Rachel is unable to bear Jacob a son, and so, just like Sarah, Rachel "took her servant Zilpah and gave her to Jacob as a wife. Then Zilpah bore Jacob a son." In light of the actions of these "holy" people, it seems almost impossible that the rest of us are branded as sinners.

The holy books have lofty titles for Abraham (*Khalil-Ullah*, or "Friend of God") and for Moses (*Kalim-Ullah*, "the One to Whom God Speaks"). How did these titles come to exist? We don't know the behind-the-scenes true story. It remains a mystery, as Surah 3:179 tells us: "He separates what is evil from what is good. Nor will He disclose to you the secrets of the unseen, but He chooses His Apostles as He pleases." But how did they obtain these titles and why? They seem largely self-given, owing to a grandiose sense of ego. Abraham, for example, almost puts himself in the same realm as God when, in Surah 21:56, he says, "Your Lord is Lord of Heavens and earth, He created them from nothing and I Abraham am a witness to this Truth." Is he really claiming to have seen God bring the world into being? If so, then describing him as "grandiose" is mild, to say the least. The word *witness* means "one who may testify as to what took place." Needless to say, Abraham would not qualify as a witness in today's courts.

A person needs self-confidence to serve as a leader in senior management, but Abraham takes this notion a little too far. Surah 21:58 tells us, "So (Abraham) broke the stone Idols to pieces, all but the biggest of them, that they might turn (and address themselves) to it." This was a boldly arrogant move, intended to shame the people for worshipping stone idols. Abraham was an instigator who used all tools available to him to spread the word of God. He hated stone idols and performed violent acts to degrade the pagans. He knew that once he broke the statues, the pagans would turn to the surviving biggest statue and ask him how it all happened. Abraham left the biggest idol untouched and broke the others to pieces, as if a fight broke out between the idols, and the biggest had smashed rest. So after Abraham broke the statues, he added fuel to the fire by mockingly asking *the pagans* how it all happened; don't ask me! Why don't you ask the idols? Imagine asking the same question of Abraham, however. Suppose pagans had gone inside the sacred mosque of Mecca, broken the sacred stone, and then asked Abraham, "Well, who did it?" There would have been hell to pay. I would like to see how long Abraham would survive today if he entered a Hindu temple and played the same arrogant trick.

Taking this scenario a step further, let's put modern-day monotheists in the pagans' shoes and challenge them on the very point on which Abraham challenged the pagans. Abraham demanded to know how the pagans could blindly believe in idols just because their forefathers had done so for generations. In Surah 43:22, the pagans say, "'We found our fathers following a certain religion, and we do guide ourselves by their footsteps.'" It is a common cultural phenomenon that people follow the ways of their ancestors. Pagans do it, and so do monotheists. Let's go to Saudi Arabia or any Middle Eastern culture and ask the same question: "Why are you following in the footsteps of your forefathers, who believe in the Muslim religion?" This would be an offensive question which we wouldn't actually ask, but if we did, the answer would be same as pagans' answer above.

Abraham could get away with being disrespectful to the pagans, because he and God had an agreement. This accounts for some of Abraham's bad behavior. In Genesis 15:17, God says, "To your descendants I give this land from the River of Egypt to the River of Euphrates." Genesis 17:6 has God saying, "And I will make nations of you." In Genesis 17:10, God states, "This is My agreement, which you shall keep between you and Me and your offspring after you: Every male among you shall be circumcised." The question is, why circumcision? Certainly, the practice had been around for a long time. Historically, Abraham was not the first male to be circumcised. Pictures of circumcision can be found in temples, in paintings three thousand years old. The practice of circumcision has been on a start-and-stop roller-coaster ride ever since, depending on social and political dictates. But it involves the most sensitive, private part of the male sex organ—and God wanted this cut in exchange for land? What would be the response of the president, people, and pope today if God offered us a similarly absurd deal? Suppose God agreed to end the violence in Iraq and Syria in exchange for all of us chopping off our ring fingers.

Some Greek and Jewish philosophers made circumcision more appetizing by introducing the notion that a circumcised penis looks as healthy and clean as a heart. But like any new law, trend or fashion, circumcision had its pros and cons. The local Greeks found it highly offensive; King Antiochus therefore banned the practice. The Apostle Paul's teachings led the gentiles to believe that if you have faith in Jesus Christ, there is no need for circumcision. In the Book of Jubilees 15:27, the angels are already circumcised! (The *Book of Jubilees*, sometimes called the "Lesser Genesis," was written around the second century BC and records an account of biblical history of the world from creation to Moses.) Angels are spiritual beings. Do they really have penises? If so, are they symbolic or functional? These questions suggest that the writers of the holy books often forgot that they were writing about heavenly entities, not human beings.

At any rate, Abraham entered Egypt not so much to spread the Word of God, but to ensure the survival of his family, as the Nile had plenty to offer for many migrants. Genesis 12:10–11 tells us that "Abraham went to Egypt to live there as an alien, for famine was severe in the land.

When Abraham was about to enter Egypt, he said to his wife Sarah, 'You are a beautiful woman. The Egyptians might kill me but keep you alive for themselves. Say to the Egyptians, you are my sister, not wife, and my life will be spared on your account.'" To secure his own survival, Abraham's brain began working deceitfully. He thought that his friend God would come to rescue him. Then again, this same friend had asked for the sacrifice of his son Isaac. Oddly enough, when God decreed that sacrifice, Abraham showed no sorrow. He promptly began to carry out God's orders; it was not his neck on the line. It seems that Abraham may have had sociopathic tendencies. In the end, God spared the life of Isaac, and Pharaoh spared the life of Sarah and let her go free. Abraham tricked Pharaoh with his lies, and in exchange, Pharaoh made Abraham rich by giving him oxen, sheep, and donkeys. In this case, Pharaoh appears to be more of a victim than Abraham.

Human nature reveals that if we can get away with stealing the cookie from a cookie jar once, we will try it a second time. With King Abimelech, Abraham fell into the usual pitfalls of human nature, repeating the same lie about Sarah being his sister. King Abimelech of Gerar sent and took Sarah. Verse 20:3 of Genesis tells us that "when living in Gerar as an alien, God came to King Abimelech in a dream, and said to him, 'You are about to die because the woman you have taken; for she is a married woman.'" Here again, King Abimelech becomes the victim, and God threatens the king, not Abraham, for his actions. But there is no mention anywhere of advice, counsel, or a rebuke to Abraham for spreading lies and hoodwinking people in authority. This friend of God told lies whenever it suited him. Of course, *God* chose Abraham as a messenger and a trusted friend. God handpicked Abraham for no other reason than the fact that Abraham hated idol worship.

It was Abraham's mischievous nature to provoke the pagans by burning the gods in the House of idols. When someone plans to burn a building, he makes sure he does not become a victim of his own plan; he manages to escape the instant he lights the match. But God did not save Abraham from the fire; Abraham saved himself by his own deviousness. Unfortunately, Abraham set the scene for Haran to become a victim; he knew Haran would go running into the fire to save the House of Idols. So what price did Abraham pay for the sin of killing his brother? The answer seems to be: Abraham got off scot-free! This suggests that the stories in the holy books were written by humans and not God. Holy messengers taught and spread the message of God devotedly and passionately. But soon after their deaths, scholars twisted the meaning of their message to suit the needs of religious leaders. Those leaders needed the rest of the world to get in line with their specific interpretation of God's message, so the writers tweaked a few verses or chapters here and there to bolster their positions, creating their own versions of "truth." They adjusted various terms, plots, and characters throughout scriptural history, fixing it so God came to Abraham's rescue, Qur'an 29:24: "God saved him from the Fire: there truly are signs in this for people who believe." But had Jesus humiliated and tortured on the cross for hours in front of thousands of people. And so it becomes a little difficult to believe Surah 14:47, which says, "Never think that God would fail His Apostles in His promise."

After Haran's burial, Abraham's father, Terah, moved to the land of Canaan with his family to avoid more altercations with the pagan villagers. There Abraham found God. Does this sound a little familiar, like the story of Moses, who found God after killing a man and escaping from the land of the pharaohs? The two holy messengers, the ones closest together in time, had blood on their hands but somehow managed to find God. Was this a qualification for becoming Khalil-Ulla and Kalim-Ulla in the old times? Then again, we know from the Qur'an that God picks and chooses whom He will. Ironically, omniscient God watched all this activity from His throne in Seventh Heaven, and in hiding. He did not take any initiative to guide His messengers or help them explore their new worlds. Vasco da Gama, Ibn Battuta, and Christopher Columbus went out on their own to explore the world. These explorers and travelers appeared during the fifteenth century, a time lapse of nine hundred years after the "last messenger," Muhammad. God must have wanted to keep His holy messengers on a small plot of land, where they were easier to control.

Let's take another look at Moses and how he fared as a specially chosen messenger. It appears that Moses let his followers fall to the bottom of the list of spiritual journey, letting them roam for forty years and then abandoning them to go and speak with God on Mount Sinai. According to the holy books, however, Moses freed the Israelites from Pharaoh's evil claws, guiding them through the high and low tides of the Red Sea. By this time, Moses's followers didn't have the patience to wait another forty years to see the end result of this meeting between him and God. So they started making their own golden calf for worship, as Surah 7:148 informs us: "The people of Moses made, in his absence, out of their ornaments, the image of a calf for worship." When Moses found out about the idol, he flew into a rage, dropping and breaking the tablets with the Ten Commandments written on them—the ones God had just given him. He even pulled out his brother's hair. That kind of behavior doesn't inspire much confidence in Moses's leadership abilities. As a manager, Moses is not a Six Sigma kind of guy.

Speaking of Moses's inappropriate rage, Surah 28:15 clearly depicts the scene in which Moses murders his countryman: "And Moses found there two men fighting, one of his own religion and the other, of his foes. Now the man of his own religion appealed to him against his face, and Moses struck him with his fist and made an end of him. Moses said: 'this is a work of Satan: for he is an enemy that manifestly misleads, and O Lord I have wronged my soul! Do you then forgive me?'" Of course God forgives Moses, completely ignoring a previous edict found in Leviticus 24:13: "Anyone who kills a human shall be put to death."

Moses escaped from the altercation scene and settled in Madyan, having impressed the daughters of a village chief at a watering place. Moses sounds like a smooth guy; he must have had all kinds of excuses for how he happened to show up there. First, he kills someone with whom he disagrees on the road. Next, he puts the blame on Satan. Then he has the nerve to ask forgiveness of God. After that, he runs away when he gets the heads-up that Pharaoh's men are looking for him. He later finds God in a burning bush, despite the bloodstains on his own resume. As the father of all con artists, Moses managed to use his knowledge of certain tidal peculiarities, appearing to part the Red Sea, and gave himself the title of Kalim-Ullah, the one to whom God talks. Con artists always stay one step ahead of all games, to beat the odds. If killers today followed in Moses's footsteps, blaming Satan for their misdeeds and avoiding trial in their county courts, they would all be running loose. But one thing is for sure: today's public would not accept any of God's holy messengers. Killing someone with whom you disagree, blaming Satan, and then asking for forgiveness from the Lord will not go far in the modern court system. At the very least, anyone who claimed that "the devil made me do it" would be mandated to undergo a mental evaluation.

We are told in Surah 19:51 that "Moses ... was specially chosen, and he was an Apostle and a Prophet." What devious, shifty lowlifes God selected to spread His message! It's no surprise that people had a hard time trusting these messengers. God does not mention why Moses was so special; apparently it's enough that God chose him. Surah 2:108 admonishes us not to ask such questions: "Would you question your Apostle as Moses was questioned of old?" Well, sure—people had every right to question Moses about his authenticity and truthfulness. But the writer(s) of the Qur'an shifted the argument and defended Moses, a criminal, by saying that the people constantly harassed him with foolish and impertinent questions.

The holy messengers of yesterday are like the politicians of today. They all make great promises for a bright future and sugarcoat everything else, saying, "I will guide you to a holy land of milk and honey," and "Bear with me," and "I feel your pain." Moses cruised around in the desert inside a two-hundred-mile radius for forty years with six hundred thousand people, like the captain of a ship with no rudder and no steering wheel. Moses's compass needle was going in circles and taking them nowhere. People grew frustrated and fatigued, and Moses worried that someone in the crowd might stand up and claim, "I, too, have seen (or heard) God." So like any shrewd politician, he had to cover all the bases, including protecting his own life and making sure no one else took command of the ship's helm. He imposed a death penalty on false prophets, declaring that anyone else who caught sight of God would die. But let's suppose someone had claimed to see God. Wouldn't that person have to have been dead to start with, according to the afterlife theory? If you're alive and you "see God," you are necessarily lying and are a false prophet. What a brilliant way for Moses to clear all the hurdles and ensure smooth sailing until he found the Promised Land.

# 11

## Likenesses between the Ten Commandments and the Code of Babylon's Pagan King Hammurabi

The story of the Ten Commandments includes some of the most important, influential, and effective passages in the Bible. Let's look at the contents of the commandments themselves. The first three sound a little arrogant, like an introduction made by a politician, community leader, or pope. The rest of the commandments are common, logical, and humane. The Ten Commandments are comprised of 133 words and were completed in forty days. That's an average of one commandment per four days. That means each word took 7.21 hours to chisel on the stone slab. That's a lot of time. Either Moses was not an expert chiseler, or God did not provide the right tools—or it took Moses, a wanted felon, a long time to swallow the message of the Ten Commandments.

In today's world, we don't need a holy messenger to bring us commandments—and certainly not after he's been involved in a lengthy debate with God in thunder and lightning. Moses and God's meeting today would not occur on a hot, storm-struck, isolated mountain, but in an air-conditioned skyscraper in Israel. Moses would work on the project for a few minutes on his computer and go back to his followers with all God's commandments on a clean, beautiful laminated board. The meeting itself would take, at most, forty minutes instead of forty days. That's definitely not enough time for Moses's followers to start thinking evil thoughts and making a golden calf in his absence.

Surah 4:153 says, "They asked Moses, 'Show us God in public,' but they were dazed by the thunder and lightning. Yet they worshiped the calf even after clear signs ... And we gave Moses proof of authority." Is this the best proof Moses can offer for the presence of God on Mount Sinai? When lightning strikes, we become dazed, faint, or die, or tree limbs turn into ashes. Lightning and thunder are the visual and auditory crash that occurs from the buildup of electrical charges in a cloud. That is not a clear sign of God's existence. Before biblical times, a village's holy chief would explain lightning, floods, rain, and famine as indications of God's anger and His curse on the people of that village or region for their wrongdoing. That's the best logic the chief could come up with, and the notion stuck for a long time. Think for a minute about the American Midwest, which is the site of hundreds of tornadoes every year, many of which cause death and destruction to innocent people. Today's logic tells us that God has not put a curse on the people of the Midwest; they don't suffer such loss and devastation because they are less godly than the rest of the world. Suppose we replaced all the Midwesterners with God's chosen people; do you think the tornadoes would stop? The Midwest is a region where cold air from the north hits warm air from south, and that's just a fact.

Let's take a look now at some laws that predate Moses, such as those depicted in the Code of Hammurabi. Not surprisingly, likenesses exist between the early code of King Hammurabi and the Bible's Ten Commandments. The first ruler of the Babylonian empire, King Hammurabi lived around 1780 BC, about the same time as Abraham. The famous Code of Hammurabi consisted of 282 laws governing family and civil life, criminal punishments, and prices and trade.[53] A carving portrays Hammurabi receiving the laws from the god "Shams" because he was chosen by the gods of his people to bring the law to them. Does that sound rather like another man, Moses, who existed four hundred years later and was chosen by another god, "Yahweh"? The old kings and holy messengers had certain goals in common, much like today's

---

[53] "Code of Hammurabi," *Wikipedia*, last modified October 5, 2014, http://en.wikipedia.org/wiki/Code_of_Hammurabi.

leaders: to restore order, stability, justice, and peace in their regions. The majority of the players in the leadership game kept the power ball tight in their fists until their natural deaths, trying to avoid being dethroned by another, stronger player. This power game has been going on like a revolving door for thousands of years.

# 12

## HOLY MESSENGERS, KINGS, AND POPES HAVE PULLED SIMILAR DECEPTIONS

Despite some trials and tribulations, Muhammad arguably had the easiest time of all God's holy messengers. Muhammad was a humble man who tried to find common ground with common folks and often compromised when others disagreed with him. In Surah 18:110, we hear him say, "I am a man like you, but the inspiration has come to me through God." As the messenger's voice changed with time, so did God's. The prophet Muhammad changed slowly, until ultimately he tried to be a jack-of-all-trades. Although modest and unassuming, he became a shrewd politician and a ruthless military leader; he'd always been a wise planner. A strong example of his shrewd side can be found in the story of Khaybar.[54] It is the name of Oasis 93 Miles north of Medina (Saudi Arabia). Battle of Khaybar was fought in the year 629 between Muslims and Jews living in oasis of Khaybar. Muhammad sent out his delegation to entice a new leader, Usayer, to come to Medina to meet him for a leadership role in Khyber. Usayer arrived with a delegation of thirty men. Having been double-crossed by Usayer in some manner (according to some accounts), the Muslims turned on their guests and killed them all. Muhammad could play the role of either a fierce warrior or an accomplished diplomat, depending on the situation. He also had some character flaws, like anyone else. It seems his main area of weakness

---

[54] Joseph Katz, "The Prophet Mohammed: A Jewish Pseudo-Messiah," 2001, EretzYisroel.org, www.eretzyisroel.org/~jkatz/theprophet.html.

was women. Humans love to find justifications for their behavior within the bounds of existing moral, legal, social, and religious rules—usually by putting a new interpretive spin on words. Most of the time, our behavior does not pass the test, although we try our best to defend ourselves, right or wrong, with all the tools available to us. Kings, holy messengers, popes, and community leaders play the same game with the same passion, against all odds.

Muhammad was highly interested in his adopted son's wife, Zaynab. He knew he couldn't just claim her for himself, so he started laying the groundwork for future marriage. The following verses from the Qur'an illustrate how Muhammad cleared the way to marry her. Surah 33:4 reads, "Nor has He made your adopted sons as your sons. Such is speech by your mouths ..." Surah 33:37 states, "When Zaid had dissolved his marriage with her, with the necessary formality, We joined her in marriage to you. So in future, there may be no difficulty to Believers in the matter of marriage with wives of their adopted sons ..." And Surah 33:38 asserts, "There can be no difficulty to the Prophet in what God has showed to him as duty ..." Muhammad was now able to marry Zaynab, but he harbored guilt over manipulation of the rules, and so he was eager to show that his marriage to his adopted son's wife was a *duty*. In the skillfully crafted verses above, the Quran's writers showed the followers of Islam that Muhammad was right in his decision to marry Zaynab. The writers got Muhammad off the hook, as it were. The prophet Muhammad and God worked together whenever his personal likings were outside the norm. Aisha, one of Muhammad's wives, once remarked to him, "God comes to your aid rather conveniently when it is a question of your cravings."[55]

Humans love to twist and turn legal, social, and religious rules to their own advantage and label them as permission granted from a higher spiritual authority. These maneuverings worked well in the olden days for kings, popes, and holy messengers, because people were willing to accept their authority with blind faith. Despite loving to bend the rules, however, people take matters of marriage and propriety quite seriously.

---

[55] Ibn Warraq, *Why I Am Not a Muslim* (Prometheus Books, 2003), 303.

Certain issues can cause public furor and must be dealt with delicately. A prime and famous example of bending the rules occurred in the sixteenth century and changed the course of history. King Henry VIII of England went to the pope seeking to dissolve his marriage with Catherine of Aragon.[56] Henry had become infatuated with another woman and wanted her for his new bride, but the Catholic Church did not allow divorce. Henry concocted reasons to have his marriage annulled, as annulment was the only legal option in the church. Ironically, earlier in his monarchy, King Henry had received the title of Defender of the Faith for being such a model Catholic. Now he found himself dangerously on the outside of the pope's good graces.

King Henry's wife, Catherine, had given birth to six children, all of whom died in infancy. Henry wanted a son to become heir to the throne, but Catherine was now beyond childbearing years. In order to have another child, Henry chose twenty-year-old Anne Boleyn as his new queen and the bearer of new royalty. But Catherine's nephew, the king of Spain, threatened to invade England if the pope annulled Henry and Catherine's marriage. Eventually, the pope refused King Henry's demands. As a result, the Defender of the Faith became bitterly enraged. In a stunning, historic move, King Henry declared *himself* supreme head of the Church of England and cut all ties with "the pope of Rome." It was a bold move to go against the supreme authority of the Catholic Church. This is just one high-profile example among many instances of power struggles between religious and civil leaders. It's no accident that few documents and records remain today regarding Henry's political maneuverings. In order to protect their interests and fulfill their wishes, holy messengers, popes, and kings were careful to omit certain pieces of information, leaving a particular paper trail that showed them in a favorable light. Since biblical times, many other crafty kings, popes, and other characters have pulled similar tricks, such as King David, King Solomon, and the holy messengers Abraham, Moses, and Muhammad. The holy books have put all of them on a high pedestal while covering up their pitfalls and personal foibles.

---

[56] "Wives of Henry VIII," *Wikipedia*, last modified September 26, 2014, http://en.wikipedia.org/wiki/Wives_of_Henry_VIII.

# 13

## Vague and Inappropriate Verses in Holy Books

Likewise, God himself tends to make sure He looks better and smarter than anyone else in the holy books. We see this in the story of the she-camel in Surah 7:73: "Now hath come to you a clear sign from your Lord! This she-camel is a sign unto you. So leave her to graze in God's earth, and let her come to no harm …" In this story, the prophet Salih went to the people of Thamud, on behalf of God, to spread the message of monotheism. Through Salih, God told them their job would be to pick a she-camel and let her come to no harm. Otherwise, they would be "struck by a painful torment."

Finding this "clear sign" of the right she-camel would prove pretty difficult, actually. How were the people going to find the right one? This was a hard and confusing job—like one of the Twelve Labors of Hercules, but for ordinary humans. It's quite puzzling that God, who knows all things, would send such a vague sign, and it's easy to see how the people of Thamud were taken aback, thinking this test might be a trick or a false sign. After all, God set it up to mimic a false sign, as Surah 17:59 reveals: "We avoid sending the signs, only because the men of former generations treated them as false." So God sent a mystery she-camel? Now, don't blame the people of Thamud if they couldn't distinguish between a regular camel and the special she-camel sent by God with no particular markings, sign, or other identification.

In most of the world, God continues to push His agenda, despite having won only 50 percent of the population. In the holy books, God pushes himself to the number-one position. Consider the Qur'an, in which the prophet Muhammad is commanded to speak or read the verses. These verses typically begin with the word *Say*. Here are a few examples:

- Surah 2:136: "Say, We believe in God and the revelation given to us, and to Abraham, Ismail, Isaac, Jacob and the tribes, and that given to Moses, Jesus, and that given to all Prophets from their Lord …"
- Surah 3:12: "Say to those who reject faith: 'soon will you be vanquished and gather together to Hell, an evil bed indeed to lie on.'"
- Surah 3:15: "Say: Shall I give you the glad tidings of things far better than those? For the righteous are Gardens in nearness to the Lord …"
- Surah 3:29: "Say: Whether you hide what in your hearts or reveal it, God knows it all …"

There are about 150 verses like these, starting with the word *Say*, in the Qur'an. The word looks like a tyrannical command indicating what God wants believers to say. To be sure, not saying what God wants you to say can cause great problems. The theme of fear and punishment for rejecting God runs throughout the Qur'an. God labels anyone who does not believe in Him as inferior and liable to meet a wicked punishment, as we see in Surah 6:39: "Those who reject our signs are deaf and dumb." Surah 4:56 is even harsher: "Those who reject our signs, we shall soon cast into the fire: as often as their skins are roasted through, we shall change them for fresh skin, that they might taste the penalty." This is a particularly low-level, grotesque, and ungodly approach to whoever rejects His signs. In fact, human beings often use the same approach. We tend to call anyone who disagrees with us "stupid," a "troublemaker," or a "rebel." We use every excuse to disassociate from them. Your average Joe cuts off social ties with his friends or neighbors if they disagree with him on certain points. A king might try to subdue an adversary first, but if that doesn't work, he will be ready to chop off his head.

Here are a few examples of modern leaders who were ostracized for rebelling against the status quo: Mahatma Gandhi, Yasser Arafat,

Nelson Mandela, and the Burmese leader Aung San Suu Kyi. Imperialist powers labeled all of them as troublemakers, rebels, or *naked Fakir* (an Arabic term for ascetics who live off alms). They all risked their lives to promote independence and justice for their people, and they paid the price: they went to jail, hid in lonely confinement for most of their lives, or were assassinated. One would think God might favor them. After all, He is supposed to stand for what's right, like freedom and justice.

In biblical times, God acted more like a plantation owner, endorsing and propagating slavery. Exodus 21:21 states, "For the slave is the owner's property." Surah 16:75–76 explains the dynamic this way:

> God set forth the Parable of two men a slave under the domain of another. He has no Power of any sort; and the other a man whom we have awarded goodly favors from us, and he spends thereof freely, privately and publicly: are the two equal? By no means. God set forth the Parable of two men: one of them dumb, with no powers of any sort; a wearisome load is he to his master: whichever way he directs him, he brings no-good. Is such a man equal to one who commands justice, and on a straight path?

These verses from holy books clearly show acceptance of slavery, a degrading and disgusting practice. Scholar Yusuf Ali notes regarding Surah 16:76 contain no condemnation of slavery. Imposing one's will and establishing dominance over others has been a natural part of human behavior from the beginning of time. We love to impose our religion, culture, and language on strangers. We think our way is better. In biblical times, those who used slavery as a means of seeking power and prestige received God's ultimate sanction. There it was in black and white, sanctioned in a holy book: slavery was not only permissible, it was condoned by God.

The earliest records of slavery trace back to the time of the Code of Hammurabi. This code worked conveniently for slave masters for nearly four thousand years. Kings, communities, countries, and religions accepted the practice openly and with a cavalier attitude. Throughout history, gods, holy messengers, popes, and preachers have screamed for justice, equality, and fairness in many social matters, while conveniently overlooking the horrible reality of slavery. Slowly the tide began to turn against slavery with the Enlightenment, the Industrial Revolution, and the dawn of Marxism. These social factors broke down old barriers of tradition, faith, and authority. They helped reform society with reason and logic. Today, slavery is officially abolished in all countries and regarded as an immoral and wicked act. However, it continues to exist more covertly under the guise of housekeeping, nanny services, and all prisons.

Regarding matters of justice, a rather shocking difference exists between God's version of justice and human justice. Today, criminal justice comprises three main parts: law enforcement, through which the alleged offender first faces the police; due process through the courts, during which (at least in theory) a fair and impartial jury decides the accused's guilt or innocence; and the punishment phase. Despite its well-known flaws, the human justice system, in and of itself, typically contains all the necessary steps that allow for the fair handling of the offender, the victim, and society. In contrast, God's version of justice appears much less streamlined and certainly less fair. When Eve defied God's orders by eating fruit from the Tree of Knowledge, it was due in large part to her natural human curiosity—imparted to her by none other than God Himself. So God implants in humans the desire to explore and experience, and then rebukes them when they act in accordance with their very nature. Incensed by Eve's blunder, God said to her, "I will increase your pain in childbearing; in pain you shall bring forth children" (Gen. 3:16). God didn't just punish Eve individually; he punished all females, who would suffer the pain of childbirth from that point on. How did God come to this thoughtless and reckless response? Eve did not attempt to chop the tree down; she only tasted its fruit. By today's standards, God acted out of spiteful anger, and therefore unfairly.

A more bizarre example of God's style of justice is seen in Deuteronomy 23:1–2: "No one whose testicles are crushed or whose penis is cut off shall be admitted to the assembly of the Lord ... Those born of illicit union shall not be admitted to the assembly of the Lord. Every tenth generation, descendants shall be admitted to the assembly of the Lord." These verses sound insane and impractical. One line in particular, regarding the one "whose penis is cut off," causes the most puzzlement. Is this a reference to the circumcised, despite the practice having been sanctioned—indeed, enforced—by God earlier in history? Anyway, to keep God happy and keep moving forward, let's assume a circumcised penis is a sacred one and a "cut-off" penis is a naughty one. Unlike human beings, God makes laws but does not provide proper guidelines for their implementation. Do we have to put a sign at the entrance of the assembly of the Lord that reads, "No Admission to Anyone with Crushed Testicles and a Cut-Off Penis"? If that does not work, the only other alternative would be to arrange for full-body scans, similar to those performed at most airports.

An illicit union is one defined as "not allowed by law" and therefore illegal. It also involves actions that are immoral. The next factor to understand is who is imposing this law. Is it the law of the Lord, tribe, country, religion, or culture? What's considered perfectly moral behavior in one culture can be a matter of life and death in another. A good example is the acceptance of nude beaches in France versus the requirement that women wear head-to-toe body coverings in Saudi Arabia. Public nudity in Saudi Arabia could well be punishable by death for women; it's certainly worth a couple of thousand lashes for men.[57] Is a pagan marriage illicit in the eyes of Christians and Muslims? So who decides who has permission to enter the assembly of the Lord? It appears these matters are to remain a mystery.

---

[57] "2000 Lashes of the Whip and 10 Years in Jail for 'Naked Dancing' in Saudi Arabia," FreePress.org, 2013, http://freepress.org/article/2000-lashes-whip-10-years-jail-naked-dancing-saudi-arabia.

# 14

## LUST, LOVE, AND INCEST

Speaking of mysteries, here is a tough one to solve. In Genesis 4:17, we learn that "Cain knew his wife, and she conceived and bore Enoch." This should strike us as odd, because there is no reference to any female but Eve in the book of Genesis so far. In fact, after Abel's untimely death, there were only three people left: Adam, Eve, and Cain. Where did Cain's wife come from, and what was her heritage? Interestingly, Genesis 4 and 5 clearly give the names and even the precise ages of everyone at the beginning of civilization, from Adam's descendants to Noah and his sons, but the missing link is Cain's wife, whose name and age are omitted. This necessarily leads to the taboo subject of incest, which was acceptable in biblical times, according to Genesis 20:12: "Besides, (Sarah) is indeed my sister. She is the daughter of my father but not daughter of my mother, and she became my wife." Another example of incest occurs in Genesis 11:27–29: "Terah was the father of Abraham, Nahor and Haran. Haran died in the land of his birth. Abraham and Nahor took wives; Abraham's wife was Sarah, half-sister of Abraham, and Nahor's wife was Milcah, daughter of his brother Haran, which was his niece."

Now that we've broached the topic of incest in the holy scriptures, the field is open for a more general discussion of biblical sexuality and the moral ramifications thereof. Let's get right to it, with 2 Samuel 11:2: "One afternoon David saw from the rooftop a beautiful woman bathing. David inquired about the woman and found out that her name is Bathsheba, wife of Uriah, a soldier. David sent a messenger to get her, and she came to him, and he lay with her. The woman conceived." Remember poor Uriah, sent to the front lines all because David wanted his wife? That part comes a little later, in 11:14: "In the morning, David wrote a letter to Joab the commander. 'Set Uriah in the forefront of hardest fighting and then draw back from him, so he may be struck down and die.'" Then, in 11:26–27, we are told that "Uriah's wife made the lamentation of her husband's death. When the mourning was over, David sent and brought her to his house, and she became his wife, and bore him a son."

Another example of shady behavior occurs in 1 Kings 1:1, "David was getting old and advanced in years; and although they covered him with clothes, he could not get warm. So his servants said to him, 'Let a young virgin be sought for my lord the king. Let her lay in your bosoms, so the lord may be warm.'" So they searched for a beautiful young woman throughout all the territory of Israel and found Abishag. She became the king's attendant and served him, although supposedly they didn't become intimate. Another shady story occurs in 1 Samuel 25. Paraphrased, the story goes as follows: Nabal was a rich man in Maon with a great many sheep and goats. His wife, Abigail, was clever and beautiful. When King David heard of Nabal, he sent out envoys to ask Nabal if David could share some of his livestock. Nabal apparently had not heard of David, so he said no. King David, terribly affronted, told his men: "Everyone strap to his sword." They set out to confront Nabal about his grievous faux pas. Nabal's wife cleverly arranged to spare a few items for David's men as a kind of peace offering. Ten days later, Nabal mysteriously died. When David learned of his death, he went to Abigail and wooed her shamelessly. Abigail bowed down with her face on the ground and agreed to be his wife. These biblical stories reveal the ruthless and deviously ambitious nature of King David. Again, we see God choosing leaders whose behavior appears less than holy.

Whatever King David did out of greedy self-interest, King Solomon did out of sheer excess. First Kings 11:3 tells us that Solomon had seven hundred wives and three hundred concubines—quite a staggering number. These foreign wives and concubines were a bad influence on Solomon, leading him to follow foreign gods. God takes issue with this in Ezra 9: "Denunciation of mixed Marriages." God commanded men to divorce their foreign wives for no other reason than they were not people of God. Solomon's massive harem, then, stood in direct contradiction to the Word of God. First Kings, verse 3:1, tells us, "Solomon made a marriage alliance with the daughter of a pharaoh, King of Egypt, and brought her into the house of David." Solomon became known as the richest and wisest king in the world. God gave Solomon the gift of wisdom, but when it came to matters of love and lust, he seemed oddly lacking. His behavior made God upset, so Solomon's kingdom was divided after his death.

Of course, King Solomon did get away with having the Queen of Sheba as a bedmate prior to his death. He must have really admired her, as he "gave the Queen of Sheba every wish she expressed" (1 Kings 10:13). According to Ethiopian legend, the Queen of Sheba was famous as the Queen of Ethiopia who bore Solomon's son, making him the first Ethiopian king.[58] The Qur'an's story of King Solomon and the Queen of Sheba highlights Solomon's tricky character; it shows how he deceived her into taking a compromising position, revealing her beauty. Solomon adorned the front hallway of his palace entirely with mirrors, knowing that when Sheba entered his palace, she would become confused, thinking she had just stepped into water. In Surah 27:44, we are told that "Queen Sheba entered the palace; but she thought it was a lake of water and she tucked up her skirt, uncovering her legs." What a brazen move on Solomon's part! And yet God chose this leader to spread His Holy Word. So far He's picked drunkards, murderers, con artists, and now perverts. The only one who seemed to have any sense, oddly enough, was Jesus, His own Son. Of course, He had Jesus killed.

---

[58] "Aksum," EthiopianTreasure.co.uk, 2002–14, http://www.ethiopiantreasures.co.uk/pages/aksum.htm.

# 15

## JUDGE SAMUEL AND KING SAUL

Another one of God's unseemly characters is Judge Samuel. Let's have a look at what kind of judge he was. In First Samuel 15:32, he says, "Bring Agag, King of the Amalekites, to me." Once King Agag is before Samuel, the judge says, "As your sword has made women childless, so your mother will be childless among women." With that pronouncement, "Samuel chopped Agag in pieces before the Lord in Gilgag." This is a pretty grisly scene, reminiscent of Joshua's horrendous deeds. Samuel made sure word of his cruelty would reach far and wide. He was engaged in a power struggle with the powerful and rising King Saul, and so he was willing to go the extra mile in hopes of frightening Saul out of the race. As the balance of power shifted in the battlefields, so did the positions of judges and kings; what happened in battle was reflected in Samuel and Saul's relative positions on the power scale before their Lord. Samuel had to make sure he had the most power.

The rift between Samuel and Saul started out as follows: At one point before the start of battle, King Saul waited too long for Samuel to offer God's blessing with a burnt offering. So King Saul took the initiative and offered the sacrifice himself. Samuel, of course, considered that a slap in the face and a usurpation of his power. With the help of God's curse, Samuel condemned King Saul for taking over his priestly role. King Saul, however, slapped Samuel in the face again by overruling Samuel's judgment and sparing King Agag's life, along with some good sheep and oxen. That was it for Samuel. He not only had King Agag cut into pieces, but he made a stunning decision as a politician and turfed King Saul off his throne and gave it to David. Once again, God followed Samuel's wishes and anointed David king. Prior to this tiff with Saul, Samuel had been a highly respected and honorable judge. But now he let his human desires overtake him; he became barbaric, proceeding to carry out God's brutal orders to kill every Amalekite man, woman, and child.

Given what we've learned about God so far, this mandate should come as no surprise. We have seen the Almighty's lust for human blood and how it appears suddenly and viciously in the form of sinkholes and floods (to name just a couple of examples). The flood that Noah endured was probably minor compared to, say, Hurricane Katrina. At the time of Noah's flood, all the sinners who had rejected God's signs were killed; the ark was a sign that the people inside had accepted God's signs and messages. In the emergency crisis of Katrina, President Bush, our Sunday churchgoer, did not order FEMA to ignore atheists, pagans, and nonbelievers. If he had, the whole world would have been screaming at him. In the great flood of Noah's time, God punished all of the above by drowning them. This outrageous action would be unacceptable today. Today, we don't distinguish among atheists, pagans, popes, or preachers when it comes to saving lives. All humans are equal and deserving of rescue in the eyes of an emergency medical team—but not in the eyes of God.

# 16

## GOD'S BEHAVIOR AND HOLY
## BOOKS RAISE QUESTIONS

Since we're discussing rotten behavior, let's consider Satan once again. Surah 14:22 tells us, "and Satan will say when the matter is decided. It was God who gave you the promise of Truth. I promised but I failed in my promise to you." How does God know Satan will say the words in the above verse? God had no clue how Satan would react when God lined all the angels up and asked them to bow to Adam. Is God selectively omniscient? All the angels followed God's order to bow down except Satan, who caught God by surprise. Satan was in rebellion against God for not obeying His orders. In Qur'an 7:13, God said: "Get thee down from this: It is not for thee to be arrogant Here: get out, for thou Art of the meanest (of creature). In Qur'an 7:14, He (Satan) said, "Give me respite till the day they are raised up. In Qur'an 7:15, God said, "Be thou among those who have respite." God was so shocked that He went ahead and granted Satan respite.

Let's put this situation in modern context. All vice presidents and assistants to prime ministers follow written policies, right or wrong, as required by their leaders. Presidents and prime ministers also often befriend an employee or two along the way, sharing personal stories or even having kids on the same Little League team. There comes a day, however, when major policy disagreements between leaders and followers erupt—and suddenly the president's good friend is kicked out of the office. The same is true for God and Satan. They sang and danced to the same beat for—who knows?—eons, ages. We know that Satan topped the list of angels, although we don't hear anything about his role or purpose, and we don't know anything about his "birth" or history. Let's just say that Satan and God knew each other well enough to understand each other's weaknesses and strengths. We can only imagine that Satan finally had enough of kowtowing to God for what he considered ridiculous reasons. Perhaps he was bored with being a Goody Two-shoes. For whatever reason, Satan defied and challenged God. So why didn't God foresee Satan's reaction to the command that he bow to Adam? God's omniscient, after all. Or suppose God knew Satan would refuse. In this case, He must have created Satan intentionally, deliberately embedding flaws in his character. The result of Satan's disobedience, followed by God's relenting attitude toward him, is that all of humanity was subjected to evil. It's odd that God gave Satan such a huge break, considering how angry He was. They really must have been great buddies. So to close the story, God intentionally created a haughty and self-entitled Satan, perhaps to add intrigue to His project of human creation. Or perhaps God needed Satan to justify creating Hell as a punishment—or at least as a threat to hold over people's heads. The only other conclusion we can draw is that God is not omniscient, after all.

God often appears quirky in the holy scriptures, and His behavior raises many questions. It's ironic, for example, that as someone who has to be right all the time and who wants to control of everything, God states in Surah 2:256, "Let there be no compulsion in religion. Truth stands out clear from error." If there is no compulsion in religion, why doesn't God accept those who choose a religion other than Islam? Because that's what we see in Surah 3:85: "If anyone desires a religion other than Islam; never will it be accepted of him." We also hear God encouraging violence against nonbelievers, in Surah 9:5: "Fight and slay the pagans where ever you find them." Again, if there is no compulsion in religion, then why not let the pagans live according to their free will? Also, if it is true, as Surah 3:19 states, that "the religion before God is Islam," then why did God put Jesus, Moses, Abraham, Noah, Isaac, and everyone else through all the trouble of spreading previous messages?

We also have to wonder why God would backtrack and correct His prior statements. If what He says is perfect at any time, then why is the following verse, Surah 2:106, necessary? "None of our revelations do we abrogate, or cause to be forgotten, but substitute with something better or similar." Why would God have to substitute different words at a later time? Surah 16:101–2 also states, "When we replace one verse with another, they will say 'You are a fabricator.' Say to them, 'the Holy Ghost brought it down from your Lord.'" Did God forget something in the beginning and later realize He needed to adjust some words? Not only does He sound like a typical politician here, but His perfection seems a little lacking.

And why would God seek to confuse us about anything? We can only wonder, judging from the following two verses from the Qur'an. Surah 6:9 refers to disbelievers: "If we had made it an angel, we should have sent him as a Man, and We should have certainly caused them confusion." Surah 19:17 refers to the angel who announced Mary's pregnancy to her: "We sent to her an angel and he appeared before her as a man in all respects." So how do we human beings know the difference between another human being and an angel who appears as a man in all respects? That is more alarming than just sending a flying entity with a halo! The thought of being confronted by an angelic being leads to yet another troubling question: Why would God want to scare us?

The holy books often evoke the fear of God in us, usually to amplify His almighty power over us for the purpose of deterring sin, as the following verses from the Qur'an show:

- ✦ 5:94: "You who believe! ... That He may test who fear Him unseen."
- ✦ 5:60: "Those who incurred His wrath, some He transformed into apes and swine."
- ✦ 13:8: "God does know what every female womb bears and how much the womb falls short or exceeds. Everything is before His sight."
- ✦ 2:159: "And those who cancel the clear Signs, what We have sent down on them will be God's curse."

If we're thinking of overstepping our bounds, these verses should give us pause. No one wants to be transformed suddenly into an ape or a pig. Even more powerful is the notion introduced in the third passage listed above: God sees into our very bodies, which could be too close for comfort. This might be the best but creepiest surah to exemplify the disturbing notion of mind control, which was mentioned earlier in this book.

Regarding the issue of pregnancy, medical science has come a long way since the ancient days. Comforts, knowledge, and privileges once reserved for God and old deities are now shared by average people. Today, a small test strip shows accurately in less than a minute if a female is pregnant. Doctors can easily ascertain the time frame of a pregnancy, and they can even save babies inside the womb when complications occur. Technology correctly reveals gender and the presence of birth defects long before a baby arrives in this world.

Let's take an example of two doctors and put it to the test. First there is Dr. Joe, who tries his best with all the tools available to him to cure his patients and explain all their medical conditions. Then there's Dr. Frank, who claims to know the details of every medical treatment and the cure for any disease but does not share that information with his patients. Which doctor would you see for your health concerns? Although God knows all about pregnant females, he never shares or explains any information with them, unlike like Dr. Joe.

To add insult to injury, we hear in Surah 3:6 that "He it is who shapes you in the womb as He pleases ..." Thank the Lord for creating "normal" kids, to whom we refer as little angels. But what pleases God about creating disabled little angels? These babies have committed no crime, but because of some flaws in God's Holy Human Manufacturing Machine, many disabled children have to struggle just to be considered valuable in the world. The Creator has made the lives of these children and their families difficult for no reason.

People in the United States tend to sue medical authorities swiftly when anything goes awry with childbirth or any other health-care matter. We demand quick answers from doctors who might have made an error, intentional or not. A medical doctor saves many lives and typically earns good money, but also has to purchase massive amounts of malpractice insurance for fear of being sued. On the other hand,

God—a flawless, perfect Creator—commits many errors on purpose and with no accountability. He does not take responsibility for His mistakes, and there's no insurance to compensate us for them. If we human beings didn't have to answer for our mistakes, this world would be in complete chaos. Those who believe in God as perfect and all-knowing should expect better from Him. Neither the Qur'an nor the Bible gives us any instructions for how to demand answers from God or where to send Him a letter of complaint. Instead, the holy books are filled with the usual mumbo jumbo and phrases from biblical times, such as "it's God's will" or "God said so." These meaningless phrases may give hope and comfort to some, but they provide no solutions.

Let's turn now to the importance of prayer for the faithful. Prayer is at the heart of every faith. Muslims are enjoined to pray five times a day, in keeping with a particular Hadith called "The Night Journey," which tells the story of Muhammad's ascent to heaven. According to the Hadith, during his stay in heaven, Muhammad held a conversation with God about prayer; they discussed how to pray and how many prayers to say each day. The Hadith shows Muhammad bargaining with God regarding the number of required prayers. Originally, God dictated an enormous number of daily prayers. Through tenacious negotiation, Muhammad gradually got God to whittle the number down, and then down even further, to five. Despite Muhammad's tremendous achievement, the Qur'an gives murky information when it comes to the required number of daily prayers. (Interestingly, there are Muslims called "Quranists"[59] who pray only three times a day, based on the highest number of prayers mentioned in the Qur'an. They believe that the only truly reliable source of information is the Qur'an because the Hadiths are too questionable in origin.) Notice the discrepancy in the number of daily prayers in the surahs below:

---

[59] "Quranism," *Wikipedia*, last modified September 11, 2014, http://en.wikipedia.org/wiki/Quranism.

- 11:114: "Establish your regular prayers at the two ends of the day and at the approach of the night."
- 17:78: "Establish regular prayers at the sun's declination till the darkness of the night and the Morning Prayer."
- 17:79: "And pray in the small watches of the morning an additional prayer for thee."
- 62:9: "When the call is proclaimed to prayer on Friday, hasten earnestly to the remembrance of God ..."

Performing five prayers a day is one of the core "pillars" (that is, components) of faith in Islam. This concrete pillar, however, appears to stand on a shaky foundation. The Qur'an makes no reference to five daily prayers. Some verses mention two prayers a day, and others, three. Still others mention more specific prayers, such as the Friday prayers in Surah 62:9, but without any indication of whether they should be added to the daily prayers. Also, none of the verses mentions exact times of day, yet Muslims are required to perform their daily prayers at specific hours, down to the minute.

In addition to being unhelpfully unclear, God seems to delight in playing both sides of the aisle between winners and losers, as noted below:

- 8:17: "It was not you who slew them; it was God ..."
- 17:7: "So when the second of warnings came to pass, We permitted your enemies to disfigure your faces and enter your temple as they had entered before, and to visit with destruction all that fell into their power."

In the first verse, we see God cleverly taking the credit with the winning team. But earlier, when the Roman emperor, Caesar Titus, destroyed Jerusalem in AD 70, God blamed believers and took revenge. God insists on all people having faith in Him alone; He punishes those who lack faith and claims to especially reward those who have faith in battle. But winning or losing a war is not the result of belief or disbelief in God. If faith in God determined the outcome of war, then pagans, unbelievers, and atheists would always be the losers. The rise and fall of peoples and nations has been a regular occurrence from the beginning of time. We have no evidence that a blessing or a curse from God factors into anyone's prosperity or downfall. Nations did not rise and fall because they lost or gained faith in God. Thirty-one dynasties of pharaohs and seven mogul kings rose and fell, and not because of their beliefs.

Let's look at Akbar the Great as an example. He committed terrible blasphemy by creating his own religion, a blend of Hinduism and Islam called *Din-i-Ilahi*, or "Divine Faith." This kind of sin should have toppled him, but Akbar the Great remained great. He tripled the size of his empire during his reign and, when he died, passed on the prosperity to his son. China is a modern-day example of the same thing: without any particular national faith in God, it has taken a central seat on the world stage in less than thirty years. In today's China, God is far, far away, hiding with Tibetan monks in the remote corners of the Himalayas.

A more recent historical example is Germany. After the Second World War, Germany was worn down to the ground, physically and financially; its currency was valued by weight. Germany came back on the world stage in less than fifty years, however, without any pat on the back from God. Likewise, the slow decline of the British Empire did not happen because Winston Churchill, Harold Wilson, and Margaret Thatcher stopped listening to God's warnings, sending Britain down to the bottom of the list of His favored nations. The most envied nation of all, the United States, did not put a man on the moon via the Vatican. And yet God seems to want to continue pushing His agenda on people, flatly ignoring America's doctrine of freedom of religion, which can be found in the US Constitution. Supreme Court Justice Hugo Black decreed that the US government cannot create a church or national religion and cannot force citizens to subscribe to any particular religion. As Supreme Court justices, Abraham, Isaac, Jacob, Moses, Jesus, and Muhammad would firmly veto the Establishment Clause of the First Amendment.

And still people go on believing in God. Surah 3:18 asserts that "there is no God but He, that is the witness of God, His angels, and those endowed with knowledge." Angels might have seen, heard, and witnessed the existence of God, but that's only half the story. Let's remember that to qualify as witnesses, we human beings have to *see and hear* proof of angels. Without such tangible evidence, a witness does not qualify to take the stand in a court of law. Surely God does not need a backup chorus of angels as a witness to His existence. But if God insists on proving His existence through angels, why not send angels that can be seen and heard on the witness stand? God Himself is an invisible character, however, and His angels are invisible witnesses that live with Him in an invisible realm, the Seventh Heaven. The whole sequence of invisible entities sort of ruins the possibility that God will prove His existence in a way that humans can ascertain. What good is a witness if the jury cannot see or hear him? God speaks to humans in the language of divine intelligence, but not in the language of human intelligence. Until God is willing to bridge that gap, how can one believe?

If nothing else in the holy books makes you leery of God, consider this passage from Surah 5:51: "Take not Jews and Christians for your friends and protectors; they are friends and protectors to each other ..." Another verse that echoes this sentiment more strongly is Surah 5:64: "He gives and spends (of His bounty) as He pleases but the revelation that cometh to thee from God increased in most of them their obstinate rebellion and blasphemy. Among them we have placed enmity. And hatred till the Day of Judgement." Horribly enough, God inspires suspicion and ill-will among His people. Note the phrasing of the first verse, which states that Jews and Christians are "friends and protectors *to each other.*" Having first established a measure of paranoia among the Muslims against Jews and Christians, God then plays the role of villain in the next passage, instigating hostility and hatred between the two friends. The two verses above clearly demonstrate that God doesn't want friendship or good will among any of them. It is hard to see how people espouse the theory that "God is love." Why wouldn't God want to facilitate love, friendship, and trust among the three religions? Instead, He pits various factions against one another, like any politician from any time period.

We are right to be wary of another one of God's unfortunate attributes: His propensity for sudden and illogical cruelty. Surah 17:101 states, "To Moses we did give nine clear signs ..." These signs are typically believed to be: 1) the rod; 2) the radiant hand; 3) the years of drought and shortage of water; 4) short crops; 5) epidemics among men and beasts; 6) locusts; 7) lice; 8) frogs; and 9) water turning to blood. These are all fairly grotesque signs, which raise the question: Is this how God proves His existence—by imposing negative, cruel, and harsh punishments on humans? The fact is that drought, water shortages, sparse crops, and plagues still exist among man and beast and will continue to appear in the future. These things are all just part of the cycle of life. Most people today do not consider these unfortunate events to be proof of God.

Surah 5:114–15 raises several interesting questions: "Said Jesus, 'O God our Lord! Send us from Heaven a table set with food that may be for us, for the first and last of us …' God said, 'I will send it down unto you: but if any of you after that resist faith, I will punish him with a penalty such as I have never inflicted on any one among all the people.'" So why would Jesus ask for a table with food from heaven? Why not simply make it appear? After all, Jesus could make his own miracles. And why would God use the table of food only as a bargaining chip to secure total allegiance? Plus we never find out if Jesus got the table of food; if he did receive it, there were no details about its shape, its color, or any of its contents; hence, only belief in God matters. Faith in God is the centerpiece of all religions, followed by outrageous threats from God if it looks like He might stray from the center of the centerpiece. We can only hope that Jesus got lucky and got his food. Faith and religion, it seems, depend on luck.

Luck was certainly a hot topic for Moses. In Surah 20:29, Moses sends out a supplication to God: "And give me a minister from my family—Aaron my brother." It's not surprising that God "granted" him his wish; Moses had already picked his brother, placed him in front of the masses as his minister, and then claimed he had God's approval. None of the holy books mentions Moses's form of communication with God—whether they spoke by hotline, telephone, fax, or telepathy, or communicated highly palpably, as Jacob did when he wrestled with an angel (who represented God) for a whole night. It was understood that holy messengers, priests, and holy men of the village communicated with God regularly; all they had to do was *claim* to. If a priest's wish came true, it was assumed to be an act of God or a sign of approval from God. If it did not, well, the priest had no reason to tell his story to the village people. Typically, we call this luck.

Here's another example of sheer "luck": Hundreds of thousands of people play the Lotto every month, and only a few win the top prizes. Most play with a firm hope or even belief that they will win, or else they wouldn't play. As usual, some pray and some do not, although most religions discourage gambling. Suppose a man of faith hits the jackpot after twenty years. He will have a field day for months to come, sharing rich stories about how God eventually answered his prayers and how he had a gut feeling that one day he was going to hit the big one. What if an atheist hits the jackpot without any supplication to God? Is that just a freebie? Do we call it God's mercy? No, we call it luck.

In Surah 2:171, God warns humanity that "those who reject faith are as if one were to shout like a goatherd, to things that listen to nothing but calls and cries: deaf, dumb and blind, they are void of wisdom." Surah 6:39 echoes this sentiment: "Those who reject our signs are deaf and dumb." *Faith* can be defined as belief obtained not with the physical senses but with a spiritual sense. Faith assembles on a shallow and hallowed ground without any reason, logic or proof. The Qur'an tells us that those who reject faith are like stupid and blind cattle. But in reality, the reverse is true. All you need do is look at the faces, emotions, and physical state of young children in the madrasas (Islamic schools) of India, Pakistan, and Afghanistan. Kids recite the Qur'an, swinging their heads to the rhythm of words, without understanding the meaning of a single one. Is that what is meant by a spiritual understanding of faith? One can reject God's words without being deaf and dumb. Rejecting God's dubious signs and laws does not make you senseless. And it doesn't kill you either. If it did, most of us would be dead for working on Saturday, a practice Exodus 31:15 forbids with the threat of death:

The Lord said to Moses, "You shall keep the Sabbath, because it is holy for you, anyone who profanes it shall be put to death; whoever does any work on the Sabbath day shall be put to death." The Sabbath is considered a holy day in several religions, based on the notion that the Lord made heaven and earth in six days and rested on the seventh day. According to the Qur'an, all God has to do is say, "Be," and it is. Somehow, "Be" turned into six days of hard labor, which turned into fatigue, causing God to rest like human beings. Dear God! You had no clue that twentieth- and twenty-first-century generations would become entrenched in a twenty-four-hour-a-day, seven-day-a-week work ethic? That's become the norm in the United States in order to secure anything like a future. Next, the biblical punishment (the death penalty) for breaking the Sabbath law is unduly harsh. The zealous application of the Sabbath law today would shrink the world population from six billion to six thousand overnight. So often God seems out of touch with the reality of the times, and His punishments don't match the crimes. Interestingly, Jesus himself broke the Sabbath law out of compassion for a crippled man. He healed the man, explaining, "My father has never yet ceased his work, and I am working too" (John 5:18).

Fishing was a common profession in Jesus's day. Fishermen had to have patience to catch enough fish to survive. In today's world, fishing is not solely a survival tool; it's also a hobby, with advanced technology and no sacred revelations from God. Fish will take bait on any day, Sabbath or not. Jesus's first disciples, Simon, Andrew, James, and John, were fishermen; Jesus called them to abandon their nets and "fish for people" instead, as part of his ministry. Muhammad's ministry, however, bears no evidence of fishing, fishermen, or any kind of water, because Mecca was set squarely in the desert! Parables in the holy books always match the environments of the people for whom they were intended; in order to truly relate to the stories, people had to have had the same kind of experiences as the characters in them.

The life stories of Jesus and Muhammad suggest that they also performed miracles—perhaps not as deviously as Moses, of course. Magic, myths, and miracles were part of everyday life in biblical times. In today's world, magic has taken a backseat; it has been relegated to shows. A certain section of society still views magic with fascination, and a fair number of people flock to see the wonders of the David Copperfield show in Vegas. If Copperfield had a chance to pit his skills against those of Pharaoh's sorcerers, even Moses would get the shock of his life. Let's take a look at Moses's miracles in Surah 26:43–45: "Moses said to them:

'Throw you, that which you are about to throw!' So they threw their ropes and their ropes and rods … Then Moses threw his rod, when, behold, it straightway swallowed up all the falsehoods which they fake!"

The story of Moses and Pharaoh's sorcerers throwing rods is a typical old mythical story. They tried to outsmart each other by whatever mystical powers were assumed to be available to them. Pharaoh's men used magic, whereas Moses mostly talked a good game, speaking in mysterious terms about God. Moses relied on spiritual powers, an older version of modern magic. The whole game revolved around the tricks of Pharaoh's ropes and Moses's rod. Both men used the same tricks from the same magical textbook of their day. It just so happened that Moses showed himself to be the superior trickster. The Qur'an itself was designed to hype up the magician's crowds, as Surah 3:179 reveals: "He will not disclose the secrets of the unseen …" We human beings tend to be fascinated with secrets and have a strong curiosity regarding the unknown; we are prone to search for whatever's on "the other side of the curtain." Imagine if you were at a stage production of the Copperfield show and suddenly he started to explain each trick in detail. After a while you would leave your seat, feeling silly.

Miracles, myth, and magic rely on secrecy, a little bit of intimidation, and a lot of showmanship. God, David Copperfield, and the gang all share the same hallmarks: hiding their tricks in a somewhat ominous manner, reveling in all the accoutrements of their trade, and pandering devotedly to the crowds. In addition to being magical, God's Kingdom is like a supercasino where winning and losing depend on the luck of the draw, but not in the minds of the populace. To them, the casino is the great Mecca of Last Hopes. People go into casinos (and places of worship) dressed in particular colors, right foot first, or rubbing the happy Buddha. The supreme winner, of course, is the casino, except for the odd one or two players. Hope of the lucky draw makes life a little more bearable, however briefly. Religion's magic makes life easier too.

# 17

## HUMAN BRAINWASHING
## STARTS FROM DAY ONE

We are persistently influenced to accept religion, to adapt to religion, not because it is provable, but primarily because it can help people manage their lives, and it gives them a sense of future (i.e., life after death). Theoretically, everybody wins with religion. In reality, this is not true. All religions are sadly infested with complex intellectual dishonesty and moral fraud, posing a vast and false picture of spiritual rewards. As we have seen in the Qur'an, every second page makes reference to fear, punishments, and rewards—for a total of about 570 such references. It is a common supposition that honesty flows in a straight path from the holy reservoirs of religion. From childhood, we learn to view religious officials as sinless; they are special people who live in a higher realm than the rest of us. Most believers accept this notion without any concern or question. That belief rests on assumed facts without proof or full knowledge; it comes from rumors or fantasy and lives in the emotions. Most believers don't make an effort to consider the facts.

Here is one odd belief of my mother's that was practically a divine edict in our house when I was growing up: "Never ever eat watermelon and rice together in the same meal." Mother firmly believed that the interaction of rice and watermelon in the stomach would cause death. How did she get this wacky notion? We kids were brainwashed to the point that we avoided the sight of watermelon if we had eaten rice even the day before! When I left home and saw a coworker eating rice and watermelon together, it gave me the shock of my life. But the next day I saw him alive and happy, as usual. One day, with sweaty palms, I hesitantly ate watermelon and rice for dinner. To my surprise, I was up, alive and well the next day! I hadn't even suffered a stomach cramp. Now the old, scary myth about rice and watermelon is a family joke. Beliefs can be bizarre, whether they're religious, cultural, or national, and people can become highly defensive about them.

We enter this world not with a hearty laugh but with a loud cry, and we leave it with a moan and a sob. The urgency to adopt religion starts before we take our first breath in this world. Our parents make sure that we get the correct names, which we will carry with us until they're engraved on our tombstones, and these names are often religiously and culturally based. You will not find Western parents giving their child the common Arabic name Muhammad, or Eastern parents giving their child the name Peter or Paul. Parents leave us when we are middle-aged, but we carry the names they chose for us until we die. Our religious indoctrination starts at an early age to satisfy our parents' wishes, needs, longings, and pledges to their deity. This kind of upbringing does not leave much room for children to grow, think rationally, or choose their own commitments. Muslims begin introducing their newborn babies to Islam by reciting the verses of the Holy Qur'an in their ears. Jews circumcise their babies on the eighth day of life, and most Christians baptize their children as infants.

Let us now perform a very safe experiment on three newborn babies, with permission from their respective parents! Let's try reciting the Qur'an in the ears of a Jewish baby, baptizing a Muslim baby with holy water, and circumcising a Christian baby with the corresponding Jewish ceremony. This is all we will do, other than waiting for them to become adults and watching the results. I am sure that these traditional religious rituals and practices will have no bearing on the babies' belief systems later in life. Babies cannot distinguish between a surah and a Beatles' song. "Choosing" your parents' religion is a self-consoling behavior to comply with tradition. I believe that if babies could speak, their first question to their equally brainwashed parents would be "Why?" The parents would answer quickly, like a schoolteacher who does not know the right answer, "Keep quiet; you are too young to know right now."

It is ironic that parents go to such lengths to make sure their child has the "right" name, behavior, clothes, education, friends, religion, and so forth, yet they cannot think critically about their child's right to choose his or her own belief systems. Our parents tend to assign us religion selfishly and carelessly, early in our lives, while in every other respect they try to think through the consequences of their decisions about our upbringing. Deciding which religion to join is one of the most important decisions you can make. It affects how you approach and interact with the world—whether you do so blindly, with eyes closed and mind shut, or whether you critically explore a wide range of options. Consider, for example, the following surah contrasted with some lines from a poem by Khalil Gibran,[60] paying particular attention to the tone of each.

Surah 2:47:
"O Children of Israel! Call to mind the special favor I awarded on you, and that I preferred you to all other nations."

From "On Children":
Your children are not your children,
They are the sons and daughters of Life's longing for itself.
They come through you but not from you,
And though they are with you, yet they belong not to you,
You may give them your love but not your thoughts,
For they have their thoughts,
You may house their bodies but not their souls,
For their souls dwell in the house of tomorrow,
Which you cannot visit, not even in your dreams.
You may strive to be like them, but seek not to make them like you.

Unless you are tone-deaf and poetically immune, you would have to say the poem sounds more appealing than the verse from the Qur'an. The poem by Khalil Gibran is structurally and phonetically designed to

---

[60] Kahlil Gibran, *The Prophet* (Alfred Knopf, 1988), 18–19.

evoke a sense of openness and balance. Which one better reflects the way in which you would rather judge the world? Imagine growing up reading only texts that smack of harsh authority. What sort of thinker would you turn out to be? An independent and self-assured critical thinker? You would become brainwashed to respond to dictatorship.

Plato eloquently explains the phenomenon of human brainwashing in his story "The Allegory of the Cave."[61] Paraphrased, the story goes as follows: Since childhood, the men living in the cave have been shackled so that they can see only the cave's inner walls. Totally isolated from the outside world, they come to perceive the cave as a prison and the cave's shadows as guards. Eventually, the shadows become real people to these men, who even assign names and personalities to them. One day, a prisoner manages to break free. It is painfully difficult for him to adjust to the bright sunlight and outside surroundings, but he eventually realizes that his life in the cave has been based on falsehood. He goes back into the cave and tells the men about life on the outside, explaining that their "prison" is just a cave and that the "guards" are just shadows. The story's meaning, of course, is that our perceptions are limited; we unknowingly live in a small place of illusion, creating our own reality. Likewise, in today's world, our days are spent learning the illusions we're expected to believe. Our teachers and parents reward us for holding fast to these illusions. In many respects, our lives are made easier by the ideology we have accepted. To choose freedom, we have to break the chains of delusion.

All people are cave dwellers at some point in life, including the holy messengers of biblical times—Abraham, Moses, Jesus, and Muhammad—and even the political figures of modern times, such as Martin Luther King Jr., Mahatma Gandhi, and Nelson Mandela. Moses stood face to face in battle with mighty Pharaoh, with the monotheistic God by his side; in modern times, Gandhi faced the mighty British Empire, supported by a much more eclectic view of faith. Both achieved the same goal of liberating people.

---

[61] "Allegory of the Cave," *Wikipedia*, last modified October 7, 2014, http:// en.wikipedia.org/wiki/Allegory_of_the_Cave.

The result of growing into adulthood is that we live our lives between stories, as it were—bound by what our parents taught us, but with the growing awareness of a self that responds to the poetry of Khalil Gibran and understands what it means to break free of delusion. For thousands of years, parents have made strenuous efforts to make their children think, act, and behave according to traditional moral and cultural codes. Children, in turn, have largely accepted their parents' strict interpretations of religion and dutifully followed the ethical and moral codes of family and culture. When we reach adulthood without having evaluated our own beliefs against those of others—or against the whole gamut of potential beliefs—we become expert at condemning anyone who does not meet our narrow expectations of what is "good" or "normal." The names of the God or gods that people believe in may differ, but the characters in religious books and results are nearly the same.

# 18

## THOMAS AQUINAS, SAINT AUGUSTINE, AND ANSELM OF CANTERBURY

At some point, we have to ask the question, "Why were the thinkers, the religious leaders, and some philosophers of the past so hell-bent on proving the existence of God and original sin with nebulous words like *soul, spirit,* and *holy?*" The answer is, of course, that they needed God to confirm the validity of their worldviews and way of life, which they deemed "good" and "normal." Without God, their whole world would fall apart. A whole slew of philosophers, therefore, tried diligently to "reason" with society about God's existence. Around the middle of the thirteenth century, Thomas Aquinas asserted that the existence of God could be proven in five ways—through an understanding of motion, cause, contingency, perfection, and order.[62] His Theory of Motion states that a driving force moves everything, and that if you go back far enough in time, the "primary mover" is God. In Aquinas's day, that explanation may have been enough to satisfy people's minds regarding the existence of God. But why not go a step further and ask, What is the driving force that created God? How far back is far enough to find the original primary mover? Do we go back gazillions of years to trace the existence of God? No, we don't—because no matter how far back we go, the question

---

[62] Theodore Gracyk, "St. Thomas Aquinas: the Existence of God can be proved in five ways," Web.MNState.edu, last modified 2004, http://web.mnstate.edu/gracyk/courses/web%20publishing/aquinasfiveways_argumentanalysis.htm.

still remains: Who or what set God in motion? The fact is, if God exists, it would be easier for Him to show up and remove all doubt about His existence; after all, being omnipresent, God should be able to appear in any part of the world at any time. That way, we human beings wouldn't have to search painstakingly all over the planet or universe for an answer we simply cannot produce.

Aquinas's second argument for the existence of God, the Theory of Cause, asserts that for each event that occurs, there must be a cause—and that if you go back to the "first" event ever, you will find God. We are still in the same pickle as before, with the issue of motion. Again, we have to ask, "Who or what caused the creation of God, and what is meant by 'first'?" Humans created the concepts of "first" and "last." The numbers one, two, and three are also human constructs. What precedes the number one? Is it zero? Or minus one? So did God first exist in the time frame of minus one, minus two, minus three, etc.? Do we have to keep going through the minuses to arrive at the "first?" How would we know when to stop? How, indeed, is the term *first* defined in this case, and who defines it? Religious leaders like Thomas Aquinas—and so many other preachers, holy messengers, and popes, endowed only with limited human intellect and wisdom—relentlessly tried to define God's unlimited intellect and wisdom as beyond human reach. This is just too easy a way of saying, "I don't know."

Next, we must look at Aquinas's Theory of Contingency, which states that many things in the universe either exist or do not exist, and so if there were a time when nothing existed, nothing would exist now. Therefore, there must be a "necessary being" whose existence is not contingent on any other being. This necessary being is what Aquinas called God. According to this theory, God came out of nothing infinite years ago with His own need to be. If this is true, then isn't it possible that another (maybe even bigger and better) God could pop up out of nowhere in the future? The new God would be similar to the last God in that it came out of nowhere with no identity and gave no reason for its existence except that it had its own hidden needs and wishes. If God came into being an infinite number of years ago out of nothing, and just for His own sweet reasons, why couldn't the same thing happen again with another God? It is reasonably possible under Aquinas's Theory of Contingency!

Next, Aquinas's Theory of Perfection contends that varying degrees of perfection exist in the universe. Perfection, therefore, must have a highest form, and that form we call God. This notion of perfection, however, is a hard sell, given that a perfect God has sent many a messy disaster to earth, intentionally or accidentally, since the beginning of time. Thousands of innocent people have died in floods, famines, and earthquakes—all created by the Perfect God of Aquinas, and for no discernable reason. If Thomas Aquinas considers God to be perfection, then what is a flaw? That's like decorating a thief with medals for honesty!

Thinkers and philosophers like Aquinas, as well as the holy messengers, have portrayed God as perfect from the beginning. The many flaws of God run parallel to the so-called perfection of God, visible in the universe and on earth. Trillions of asteroids, big and small, run loose in the vast universe—and because of some mistake by the perfect controller of the universe, asteroids occasionally strike the earth, causing widespread destruction. Where is the paradigm of perfection, then? In earlier times, people assumed that objects falling from the sky indicated God's wrath. Today, we hardly ever hear someone exclaim, "God is mad!" when a comet passes by. Humans now rely on science to understand the events of space.

Last on Thomas Aquinas's list is the Theory of Order, which asserts that anything that appears to reflect a sense of purpose requires the aid of a "guiding hand"—that is, God. According to Aquinas, people, animals, and even inanimate objects such as planets have a sense of purpose because they move so perfectly in accordance with the purpose God gave them. He argues that God must have created everything with this sense of purpose. We have to remember that the thirteenth-century intellect depended on the human eye for raw data collection only. Aquinas saw the sun rise and set and called this "the order of the universe." In today's world, the Hubble Telescope has radically changed our sense of universal order. Similarly, our earth has tectonic plates that shift and move the continents, causing terrible devastation in the form of earthquakes.

Seismological evidence—of which Aquinas knew nothing—supports this observation. All is not ordered perfectly after all.

Somewhat similar to Aquinas in thinking, the renowned English Benedictine monk and teacher Anselm of Canterbury, who lived from 1033 to 1109, had a famous maxim: "I believe that I may understand." In his view, faith comes first and understanding the world comes second. His "ontological argument" connecting humans to the existence of God goes as follows: Having a conception of God necessitates the existence of God.[63] In other words, if you can think it, it must be. Just for the heck of it, let us substitute the character of God with the character of Tarzan and read the famous ontological argument with the substitution added: Having a conception of Tarzan necessitates the existence of Tarzan. Does the opinion of this Benedictine monk make us believe in the existence of Tarzan? These outdated ideas satisfied human brains at the time, but not so today.

One of the greatest fathers of Christianity, Saint Augustine, was able to explain divine beings but lacked an understanding of simple mathematics. According to Augustine, "The good Christians should beware of mathematicians. The danger already exists that mathematicians have made a covenant with the devil to darken the spirit and confine man in the bonds of hell."[64] In his mind, mathematicians made a contract with the devil to darken the human spirit and confine man to the bonds of hell. Because religious geniuses couldn't understand mathematics, they labeled it the work of evildoers. Saint Augustine's resume would head straight for the wastebasket if he were to apply to any modern academic institution. By what authority did Augustine explain the existence of God and wrongfully deny the facts and realities of mathematics as a course of study? His doctrine entitled "The Existence of God" stood as truth in his day and age, as people then were not fully independent thinkers.

---

[63] "Anselm of Canterbury," Wikipedia, last modified September 17, 2014, http://en.wikipedia.org/wiki/Anselm_of_Canterbury#Theistic_proofs.
[64] "St. Augustine v. The Mathematicians," https://people.math.osu.edu/easwaran.1/augustine.html.

# 19

## THE NOTIONS OF TRINITY AND TRUTH

One spiritual concept, the notion of the Trinity, became an absolute truth for Christians, yet the term *trinity* is nowhere to be found in the Bible. In Deuteronomy 6:4, we hear only of One God: "Hear, O Israel: The Lord is our God, The Lord alone. You shall love the Lord your God with all your heart, with all your soul and with all your mind …" Similarly, Deuteronomy 6:67 reads, "Hear O Israel: The Lord is our God, the Lord alone … keep these words that I am commanding you today in your heart … recite them to your children." These verses provide clear proof that the notion of the Trinity did not exist in the minds of biblical writers. The idea of "the Lord alone" stands out clearly, with no attachments to anyone else—an idea that had been running fairly smoothly.

The Trinity was not an exclusively Christian idea; it already existed in Indian, Roman, and German religions. Around AD 200, the first Latin theologian, Tertullian,[65] introduced the word *trinity* into the Christian faith, creating one of the most sacred and most controversial doctrines of the church. Two hundred years later, the Nicene Creed further bolstered the notion of the Trinity. In AD 431, two emperors, Theodosius II[66]

---

[65] "Tertullian," *Wikipedia*, last modified September 26, 2014, http://en.wikipedia.org/wiki/Tertullian.
[66] "Theodosius II," *Wikipedia*, last modified July 5, 2014, http://en.wikipedia.org/wiki/Theodosius_II.

and Valentinian,[67] confirmed the Trinity as central to Christian belief. At this point, the Trinity could not be debated; to question or speak against it was considered blasphemy, punishable by a harsh sentence ranging from injury to death. The Trinity serves as an excellent example of a human-made conception turned into blind belief. Hammered long enough into the brain, blind belief eventually becomes sacred and holy.

In the same era as Abraham, the wife of Babylonian King Nimrod first brought the concept of the Trinity to the world stage. King Nimrod was a hero in life. His wife, Semiramis, shared the throne with him, and after his death, she wanted him to be worshipped as a god. She recognized that without a posthumous elevation in power for him, she would lose her throne. She then unleashed a shrewd strategy to retain her royal stature. When Nimrod died, she was pregnant with his child, so she told everyone that her womb held none other than the reincarnation of Nimrod. That was a good start of a father-son deity, and Semiramis later completed the triangle of Trinity by adding herself as mother-goddess. She effectively and cleverly restored the Kingdom of Nimrod with this Trinitarian religion.

Plato picked up on the Trinitarian notion and wrote the Doctrine of Trinity around 4000 BC in his Phaedo. In Plato's view, the Trinity consisted of Agathon, the Supreme God or father; the Logos, which is the Greek term for "word"; and Psyche, meaning "soul, spirit, or ghost." Plato's writings conform noticeably with the Trinity of Christianity. Many earlier pagan religions also adopted a Trinitarian doctrine. As mentioned earlier, the Trinity appears in the Hindu religion as well. Hinduism is more than two thousand years old and features three gods: Brahma, Vishnu, and Shiva. These gods represent the forces of creation, preservation, and destruction, but they end up comprising one overarching God. Despite its polytheistic nature, then, Hinduism ultimately subscribes to the monotheistic "truth" of one God.

Truth involves objective facts, reality, and certainty. To say that a book contains "the truth" is to make an enormous and sweepingly general claim. The Bible, the Qur'an, the Gita, and Buddhist scriptures all share the common thematic concern of "truth." But objective truth can prove highly elusive. What one person claims as true may appear to another as an outright falsehood. One's notion of truth also typically depends on many different influences, such as physical and cultural conditions, family tradition and opinion, political pressures, and financial status, to name a few. There is no one, specific, agreed-upon definition of truth. I can say, generally, that the sky is blue and the grass is green, and people will probably agree, but if I say, "Islam is true," what do I mean? Do I mean to say that all other religions are wrong? Do I mean that every single Islamic edict, writing, and Hadith is unconditionally right? Among themselves, Muslims differ in their opinions on various religious points. The same holds true for people of any religion; Christians argue about certain matters, as do Hindus and Buddhists. Truth, then, depends entirely on perception.

Let's consider a simple scenario involving a hit-and-run car accident. The truth about the circumstances of the accident will vary according to the witnesses near the scene. Certainly, determining the guilty party and the ensuing punishment can be difficult when those determinations are based on varying accounts of the accident. We know from many court trials that the memories of eyewitnesses are often faulty at best. One witness may insist that the driver of the offending car wore a blue shirt, another witness may remember the same person wearing red, and both will probably be adamant in their testimony. This is why innocent people sometimes end up on death row: eyewitnesses are just prone to getting it wrong.[68]

If establishing the truth about a car accident is so tricky, how do humans manage to determine the truth about holy scriptures that rely so much on a long line of stories passed down generations after the original, witnessed event? And how do humans determine the truth about God, an invisible character? Jesus, Abraham, Moses, and Muhammad were all men first and foremost, and then Son of God, Friend of God, or Apostle of God second. As humans, they suffered pitfalls and drawbacks and

[68] Innocence Project, "Eyewitness Misidentification," http://www.innocenceproject. org/understand/Eyewitness-Misidentification.php

had flaws like any other person. We humans created their accompanying titles to boost their historical importance and confirm their authenticity as "holy" men. Each holy messenger also had a sidekick nearby to boost his public image. Abraham had Lot, Moses had Aaron, Jesus had John the Baptist, and Muhammad had both his wife Khadija and his father-in-law Abu-Bakr. These sidekicks also increased their messengers' morale, gave them public relations advice, and even challenged them at times regarding their purpose and reliability.

The Warren Apologetics Center provides the following definition of Christian truth: "Truth is that which is consistent with the mind, will, character, glory, and being of God. Truth is the expressiveness of God."[69] Just as there is no God without Satan (and vice versa), there is no truth without lies. Both balance the scales of the mind, will, character, and self-expression. If we deny the existence of lies, we necessarily deny the existence of truth. The word *true* appears almost three hundred times in the Bible, and *lie* appears almost a thousand times. But is God linked to truth only? We've already established that God makes mistakes. He likes to take center stage; He insists on winning every time; He doesn't always supply clear and convincing reasons for making certain demands; and He surely doesn't follow through on all His promises. The Qur'an tells us in Surah 10:35, "It is God who guides towards truth." How can we be so sure that this is correct?

To continue on the theme of truth, today we know that the earth spins on its own axis, and due to this rotation, the sun appears to move across the sky. Ancient heliocentric theory argued that the sun is the center of the universe and everything revolves around it. For centuries, religious pundits promoted geocentric theory, the idea that earth is the center of the universe. The tenets of heliocentric theory are found in sixth-century Greek writings, but the theory didn't come to the forefront until astronomers Nicholas Copernicus (1473–1543) and Galileo Galilei (1564–1642) challenged it, along with geo-centrism in general. Their teachings sent a shock wave through the religious world. Galileo invented the telescope, which he used to prove his

---

[69] W. Terry Varner, "Defining Truth," WarrenApologeticsCenter.org, last modified 2014, http://warrenapologeticscenter.org/resources/articles/miscellanea/defining-truth.html.

theory. He was ordered to refrain from holding, teaching, or defending heliocentric ideas. Shortly thereafter, things went from bad to worse for Galileo, and the shit hit the fan. The church banned him from teaching, and he was prosecuted for encouraging Copernicus's theory that the earth rotates around the sun and convicted in a court of law. Although the court spared his life, he spent the rest of it on house arrest. Galileo offered to let the pope glance through his telescope, but the pope declined. In 1993, nearly four hundred years later, Pope John Paul II somewhat reluctantly apologized for past decisions regarding Galileo's work, and he openly recognized the fact that the earth revolves around the sun.

In biblical times, the prophet Joshua would have embraced a geocentric notion of the universe, as the movement of the earth rotating on its axis nearly every twenty-four hours created the illusion that the cosmos revolved around the earth. Although, Joshua was a leader, a warrior, and was in continual communication with God, it's no surprise, then, that Joshua asked for the following power from God: "On the day when the Lord gave the Amorites over to the Israelites, Joshua spoke to the Lord; and he said in the sight of Israel, 'Sun, stand still at Gideon,' and 'Moon in the valley of Aijalon.' And the sun stood still and the Moon stopped until the nation took vengeance on their enemies" (Josh. 10:12). Joshua, of course, asked God for help to do the impossible—to stop the apparent motion of the sun and moon. In reality, he was asking for the wrong thing! He really meant to ask God to stop the earth from moving, but he didn't know that's what he needed to ask. We have to wonder what God made of this. Did God have any clue what Joshua was asking? It seems that omniscient God agreed to the false human notion of celestial movement. This is odd, considering that God could have cleared up the whole matter and told Joshua the truth about these heavenly bodies. Joshua could have had a fabulous vision or revelation and told the whole world the truth right then. That would have saved Galileo a great deal of fear and trembling too. Perhaps even God had no clue about the earth's motion. Believers of faith, as always, come to God's defense, and call numerous religious happenings "metaphorical." But somehow God made the day longer by stopping the apparently moving sun for Joshua anyway.

# 20

## SACRIFICE, FAITH, AND MOHAMMAD'S NIGHT JOURNEY

Whether we're talking about One God or the Three-in-One God, the issue of sacrifice appears alive and well in all monotheistic religions. The ritual of sacrifice is as old as the earliest known civilization in the Middle East, the Sumerians. Pagan sacrificial rituals blended into the rites of monotheistic religions and continue today. But why did God or the gods originally start with human sacrifice and then move to animal sacrifice, and then to other offerings? Why would God demand a sacrifice at all? Exodus 22:29 tells us, "You shall not delay to make offerings from the fullness of your harvest and from the seepage of your presses. The firstborn of your sons you shall give to me. You shall do the same with your oxen and with your sheep: seven days it shall remain with its mother; on the eighth day you shall give it to Me." In this verse, the key word is *give*, and it needs clarification and explanation. In the Lord's understanding, "give Me your first son" seems to equate to "give Me your oxen and sheep." In biblical times, human sacrifice came about as an extension of animal sacrifice, in response to the fear of losing God's favor. Although the Bible forbade human sacrifice, sometimes it still occurred, as noted in 2 Kings 3:27: "When the King of Moab saw the battle was going against him, he took with him 700 sword-fighters to break through, opposite the King of Edom; but they could not. Then he took his firstborn son and offered him as a burnt offering on the wall."

Even God Himself, a "friend" of Abraham, couldn't find a better means of testing Abraham's will than to demand the sacrifice of his son. Is that what friends do? This is a simple story of a father's faith, but the Bible and the Qur'an differ on the identity of the intended victim. The Bible asserts that it was Isaac, but the Qur'an mentions Ishmael. Given this kind of disparity in scriptures, how do monotheistic believers know which scripture is true? In addition to the well-known story of Abraham and Isaac (or Ishmael), one of the most distinct scriptural stories of sacrifice involves the daughter of Jephthah, a famous Israelite.

Jephthah, a mighty warrior, had a hard time in his youth. His mother was a prostitute, and his stepbrothers chucked him out of the house. He started living a lawless life, spending a good deal of time raiding and looting. He earned a reputation as a tough guy. So when the Ammonites went to war against Israel, the Israelite elders went to Jephthah for help. Jephthah agreed to take command, and then for some reason—perhaps he was overeager for a victory—he made the following vow to the Lord: When I return victorious from the Ammonites, I will make a burnt offering of whoever comes out of my house to greet me. God did not ask for a burnt offering; Jephthah took the initiative to appease God in this way. Jephthah fought spectacularly well, claimed victory, and returned home to the first person who greeted him—his only daughter. Although shocked and grieved, Jephthah carried out her sacrifice according to the vow he'd made to the Lord. Despite his fame as a warrior, he was a simple, honest man who kept his word. He took care of his country without question; he served God and his countrymen well. But in the end, he lost his only daughter out of principle. Is this the reward he deserved—to lose his daughter after being a noble fighter for God's cause? Why didn't God intervene or tell Jephthah to forego the vow to spare his only daughter?

Now let's turn to the story of Abraham. This "friend of God" was a devoted and bold leader. He took the lead in opposing pagan gods, accepted One God against all odds, and followed the Lord's instructions dutifully. One of his leadership goals was to abolish the old pagan custom of human sacrifice. As in any other story from the holy books, God never orchestrates unusual events in the presence of other people. Typically, He has His selected prophet carry out the performance. According to the Bible, as per God's command, Abraham packed his tools, saddled his donkey, left with his son Isaac and two of his men, and headed for a remote mountain. When Abraham reached a certain point, he said to his men, "Stay here with the donkey, and I will go there to worship." In keeping with his devotion to God, he built an altar and laid his son on top of the firewood. Just as he was ready to strike his son's neck with a sword, Abraham heard the angel of the Lord call to him, saying, "Do not lay your hand on the boy, for I know that you fear God." Then Abraham happened to spot a ram in the thicket, and so he killed it and offered it up instead of his son. Abraham appeased God, got to keep Isaac, and stemmed the pagan tide of human sacrifice. Everyone was a winner except the poor ram.

The stories of Jephthah and his daughter and of Abraham and Isaac raise several issues that bear further examination:

1. Did God go a little too far in testing Abraham's faith by putting Isaac's life in jeopardy? What would have happened if the angel hadn't shown up to save Isaac? Would Isaac have ended up like Jephthah's daughter?
2. Jephthah saved the Israelites from their enemies, but he received what amounted to punishment by having to fulfill the vow he'd made to God.
3. By today's standards, anyone who chooses to sacrifice his son will end up either in jail or in a psychiatric facility. He will not win Abraham's title of Khalil-Ullah—or any other title besides "baby killer."

It seems that God has no compunction about risking people's lives. Not only did He put Isaac, a mere child, at risk of execution by his own father, probably traumatizing the child for life, but He certainly jeopardized Muhammad's safety a few times—most notably during the Prophet's famous "Night Journey," which must have occurred at breakneck speed on a Pegasus-like creature and required an ascension through space. According to an Islamic Hadith, a strange, horse-like animal called Buraq carried Muhammad to heaven to meet God. We can assume that Muhammad had no saddle and no reins to hold during this journey! Let's look at what Surah 17:1 says about this adventure: "Glory to God who did take His servant for a journey by night from the Sacred Mosque to the farthest Mosque ... in order that we might show him some of Our signs ..."

This verse sounds poetic and metaphorical. God could have described exactly what He meant in terms of distance from the Sacred Mosque to the farthest mosque. Let's assume, as the academics suggest, that the farthest mosque refers to Al-Aqsa in Jerusalem, and the nearest to the Sacred Mosque in Mecca. Who added the trip to heaven? The Qur'an says nothing about an intergalactic trip to heaven. But then, the Hadiths were influenced by human minds, and humans tend to embellish. Another surah, 53:13–18, gives us a bit more information about Muhammad's Night Journey, but not much:

> And he certainly saw him at a second descent,
> Near the Lote-tree beyond which none may pass:
> Near it is the Garden of Abode.
> Behold, the Lote Tree was shrouded [in mystery unspeakable]
> His sight [of the Prophet] did not swerve, nor did it go wrong!
> He certainly saw of the greatest signs of his Lord.

Again, this surah does not actually confirm the Night Journey; it just alludes to it. We have to suppose that when Muhammad "saw of the greatest signs of his Lord," he had already been transported to heaven. God once more invites human imagination to fill in the gaps.

Although few stories come close to the spectacular nature of Muhammad's Night Journey (as we will see in more detail later), all religions, whether monotheistic or polytheistic, share strong similarities. They all share the basic underpinning of faith: that God will give people a helping hand when needed. Humans crafted this notion without the use of reason, logic, or sound judgment. How do most people define faith? If a child were to define it, he or she might say it means believing in something that isn't really true. Children have their own wisdom prior to religious indoctrination.

# 21

## FAITH, DREAMS, PROPHECIES, AND PRAYERS

We usually experience "faith" in a nonreligious way at a young age and gradually incorporate it into everyday life. Remember when you were young and your father carried you on his shoulders? You did not show any fear, but felt comfortable. You trusted your father not to drop you. You had "faith" that whenever he carried you, you would be safe. That is, past experiences of safety bolstered your sense that sitting on your father's shoulders again would be safe. A psychologist might call this "conditioning." Later on in life, we transfer such earlier experiences of conditioning from our parents onto others; we implicitly trust our teachers, leaders, priests, mullahs, and personal doctors—the professionals we consult at times of physical, spiritual, emotional, and financial pain. When troubled about money, we go to a banker, and when in physical pain, we consult a doctor. They typically listen to us, ask questions, and give us advice. We simply believe that they can help us.

Let's look at the similarities between two faiths, as evidenced in the rituals of the Muslim Hajj in Mecca and the Hindus' Kumbh Mela in India. A sea of humanity gathers in these two places. Muslims stream forth to meet Allah in Mecca, and Hindus wade down to their gods in the Ganges River. In the Saudi desert, a massive array of barefoot, bald-headed humans, partially wrapped in white cloth, prepare to purify their souls in Mecca. In India, naked, ash-smeared preachers direct the ritual bathing to cleanse people of their sins. Both sets of people face harsh environments: Muslims throng together in the hot desert, while Hindus dip into the frigid, filthy waters of the river. Both sets of devotees receive spiritual comfort from their respective sources of holy water. Muslims wash in water from the Zamzam Well, and Hindus plunge their heads into the water of the Ganges. Many of the faithful bottle these respective waters and take them home as sacred relics for family and friends.

Both the Hajj and the Kumbh Mela rituals arose from stories of strife and tragedy. Hajj celebrates and honors the trial of Abraham when faced with sacrificing his son. The use of Zamzam water also marks a tragic occurrence: Sarah and Hagar didn't get along, so God ordered Sarah to leave Hagar and Ishmael in the desert. In search of food and water, Hagar put Ishmael down on the ground, and as Ishmael's feet struck the earth, the holy Zamzam Well sprang into existence.[70]

In the Kumbh Mela story,[71] two deities, Deva and Asura, fought constantly, so Lord Krishna ordered them to stir oceans of milk in order to obtain Amrita, the nectar of immortality. Lord Krishna hoped to bring the fighting to an end by promising both parties an equal share in the wealth of immortality. However, when the Kumbha (in Sanskrit language means pitcher) of Amrita arrived, a fight broke out between the two rivals; it went on for twelve days and nights in the sky. During the chaotic scene, Lord Vishnu flew away with the pitcher of Amrita, spilling drops at four locations. Hindus still gather today at these locations to "wash away their sins."

Both stories sound as if they were born of imagination. One god created holy water, and the other holy nectar. People followed these mythical characters for generations; as a result, they gradually turned into a larger part of people's real (daily) lives. What is the best way to test the existence of God and Lord Krishna? Let's have Muslims and Hindus switch rituals, so that the Muslims go to Kumbh Mela and the Hindus go to Mecca. At the completion of both rituals, we'll see how many Muslims found Lord Krishna at Kumbh Mela, and how many Hindus

---

[70] "Zamzam Well," *Wikipedia*, last modified September 19, 2014, http://en.wikipedia.org/wiki/zamzam-well.

[71] "Kumbh Mela," *Wikipedia*, last modified September 28, 2014, http://en.wikipedia.org/wiki/Kumbh_Mela.

soul-searched and formed ties with Allah in the Sacred Mosque in Mecca. There will be logistical problems, of course. First of all, switching locations will be a hard sell, even if God and Lord Krishna agree to the idea. Second, Hindus will never find Allah and Muslims will never find Lord Krishna, because those deities exist as human conceptions fueled by imagination.

In keeping with the vividly imaginary, kings and holy messengers associated with all three main monotheistic religions paid close attention to dreams. Dreams comprised the heart and soul of ancient cultures and religions, becoming synonymous with prophecy or divine revelation.[72] The early Israelites perceived their lives as closely linked with dreams; Christians also came to embrace this view. The book of Genesis recounts many stories about dreams full of divine inspiration. Islam and Christianity have many prophets in common, such as Noah and Moses, and so dreams also play an important role in the Islamic faith. Again, we see how each religion followed the previous one in many respects.

The particular interpretations of certain dreams may have varied from one village to the next, but dream interpretation itself was a common practice. Humans possess a natural inclination to want to have things go in their favor; they interpret laws, rules, Hadiths, and even dreams to their liking or advantage. Many old civilizations used dreams as a lever of social control. The most qualified person to interpret dreams was a high priest. God, holy messengers, high priests, and the interpretation of dreams kept religions alive with the aim of controlling community beliefs and behaviors; God selected human holy messengers, and they, in turn, chose certain high priests to confirm their messages. Kings or the rabbinical Supreme Court had to choose a high priest wisely, because the two worked hand in hand; selecting the right high priest was crucial to success of both parties. Many kings and holy messengers made decisions based on a high priest's interpretation of dreams. In today's world, dreams have lost their mystical power. The interpretation of dreams has

---

[72] "Sleep Blog: History and Meaning of Dreams in Ancient Culture," Snoozester. com, last modified January 11, 2011, http://blog.snoozester.com/2011/01/13/ history-and-meaning-of-dreams-in-ancient-cultures/.

given way to the medical exploration of the sleeping human brain. No president, prime minister, or other public official makes decisions based on dreams. But during the times of the holy messengers, acting according to dreams was the rule, not the exception.

In addition to dreams, prophecy played an important role in religion—more so in the earlier stages of the religions that we recognize today. The practice of prophecy is by no means new or limited to any one culture. It was common in many early civilizations, societies, and religions. In ancient China, for example, people placed great faith in the prophetic text known as Chen. Fortunetelling was also common, as was palmistry, which predicts the future of a person by interpreting lines on the hands. Around 1614, the Falnama appeared—a book of omens given as a gift to the Ottoman sultan Ahmad I. Fortunetellers later started using it to entertain paying customers in the marketplaces of Iran and Turkey. Some cultures practiced prophecy more than others, depending on supply and demand.

In ancient times, kings had a cabinet of wise men for daily affairs, a magician for entertainment, and a fortuneteller for matters of health, wealth, power, and love. In today's world, heads of state have excellent doctors, top financial advisors, and expert political strategists available at any time. When it comes to matters of love, however, the advice available to them must be sparse, as they continue to make grave mistakes in this regard. A simple example of our penchant for prophecy today is the Chinese fortune cookie, which most people open out of curiosity, if for no other reason. Another example is the newspaper (or Internet) horoscope: many people take a quick glance at the horoscope column just for the heck of it, even if they don't believe in astrology. Prophetic observances tend to be vague and general, never offering specifics about names, places, or times. Prophecies in the Torah often contain God's overall warnings about ignoring its guidelines. There exists no verifiable way to evaluate their authenticity.

Another crucial component of religion is prayer. All religions have some set of rules or points of guidance about prayer. People pray to God in different postures, directions, and patterns, according to their respective traditions. The prayer environment vary from pin-drop silence in a mosque (between the imam's intonations) to the loudly ecstatic evangelistic practice of speaking in tongues, which often involves religious frenzy or trance states. Prayer gives a sense of importance to people and their lives. It also gives consolation. But ask yourself this question, standing firmly outside the loop of your own beliefs: Does Allah listen to prayers directed to the Bhagwan, and/or does the Bhagwan listen to prayers meant for Allah? If the answer is yes, then Ayatollah Khomeini[73] and his staunch followers should try saying their prayers in a Hindu temple. Likewise, avid followers of the Hindu faith should have the chance to pray in a mosque. If the answer is no, then many gods exist.

A quick note of interest about the Ayatollah Khomeini: His paternal grandfather was an Indian who migrated to the Iranian town of Khomein in the early nineteenth century. Some Iranians felt, and continue to feel, that his "tainted" blood meant that a true Persian was not at the helm of the revolution, the most momentous event in their country's modern history. When the time came to change the symbol on the Iranian flag from the lion and the sun, Khomeini chose a stylized form of the name Allah, which bears a remarkable likeness to the Sikh symbol. Some Iranians discredited him as a Hindi, which happens to be his grandfather's surname.

---

[73] Hooman Majd, *The Ayatollah Begs to Differ* (The Doubleday Publishing Group, 2008), 167.

# 22

## BUDDHISM

One religion we have not yet discussed is Buddhism, which stands in stark contrast to monotheistic religions. Buddhism does not recognize God in the traditional sense. Although technically polytheistic, Buddhist "gods" are more symbolic in nature; they represent aspects of the human soul and primarily aid humans in their meditative endeavors. Let's take a quick look at Buddha's life and teachings. For our purposes here, we'll need to simplify a great deal of complex information at the risk of committing reductionism.

Known as Siddhartha Gautama, Buddha was born in Nepal in 623 BC.[74] His father was a tribal chief, so he was born into a prosperous and well-known family. He grew up with all the comforts of a prince. His father wanted Siddhartha to be a great king, so he shielded the boy from religious teachings, all human suffering, and anything else that could take him off the royal course. Buddha therefore led a life confined to the palace, and all efforts were made to keep him involved in princely matters; he was to be groomed for greatness. But Buddha could not contain his longing to know the world. He became frustrated with his father's efforts to quarantine him into a life of politics, and he felt that his life was incomplete. So at the age of twenty-nine, he left the comforts of the palace and set out into the surrounding streets, among the populace. He wanted to meet his subjects personally—and meet

---

[74] "Buddhist Studies: Story of the Buddha," BuddhaNet.net, last modified 2008, http://www.buddhanet.net/e-learning/buddhism/001bio.htm.

them he did. These people were very different from himself and his family: the sick, the oppressed, the aged and infirm, and those living in squalor and poverty. Buddha found himself deeply responsive to human suffering and wanted to help people overcome their hardships. He found within himself an extraordinary wealth of compassion for his people and yearned to join them in all their struggles, delights, and tragedies. After indulging significantly in various delights, he learned of the religiously ascetic. These men shunned physical comforts and attachments, abstained from any kind of indulgence, and devoted themselves to improving and expanding their mental abilities as a way of rising above the human condition.

Buddha was drawn to the ascetics and notion of a religious life; we could say he found his calling. Rather than causing him to run quickly back to the palace, the horror he encountered on the streets inspired him to go out into the world. One of his senior idols, Brahma Sahampati (most senior Mahabrahmas), convinced him to follow the ascetic life. On this journey, he became aware of the mind's potential for higher (that is, more peaceful) states of being, and he began to seek for himself the meanings of Awakening and Truth. He quickly committed himself to the discipline of meditation and entered into an arduous forty-nine-day retreat of total poverty and deprivation. Thus began Siddhartha Gautama's path to become the Buddha.

Buddha is responsible for a plethora of teachings, but most notably, he developed the Four Noble Truths[75] that are firmly fixed at the heart of Buddhist teachings: the truth of suffering (or anxiety); the truth of the origin of suffering; the truth of the end of suffering; and the truth of the path leading to an end of suffering. Using the Noble Truths in conjunction with meditation as a lifelong guide, one can train the mind into achieving a state of Nirvana—the ultimate goal of all Buddhist thought and action. Nirvana denotes a perfectly peaceful state of mind in which one is free from ignorance, greed, hatred, and all other conflicting or tormented states of being so common to humankind. Nirvana is the

[75] "Four Noble Truths," *Wikipedia*, last modified October 4, 2014, http://en.wikipedia.org/wiki/Four_Noble_Truths.

pure stillness of mind that occurs when one lets go entirely of the world's pains, longings, passions, and distractions. For the Buddhist, aspiring to Nirvana is an individual process designed to induce a peaceful mental state, but it is also a highly social endeavor. Buddhist monks congregate together and submit to the process of achieving Nirvana as a community. They practice Buddhism for their own sakes, but also for the sake of humanity—that their balanced mental energy may ultimately improve human relations and bring about positive energy in the world.

Like the holy messengers throughout the Bible and the Qur'an, Buddha was greatly concerned about the human propensity to become overpowered by greed, ignorance, and hatred. Unlike the others, however, his focus remained on humanity, and he took a more humanistic and compassionate approach to teaching, as opposed to setting himself up as a holy messenger. Buddha's geographical location was about twenty-three hundred miles from Jerusalem, the hub of monotheism; had he been born in that region during biblical times, he most likely would have had no choice but to fall into the trap of proclaiming himself an apostle or "Messiah Buddha." But he was able to promote his personal beliefs for the total good without saying, "God said so," or having to become the special friend of an exclusive God. If human beings were to follow Buddha's path sincerely and genuinely, they wouldn't need to rely on the conception of a self-centered and self-applauding God. They would rely instead on their own mental and emotional resources. Jesus Christ could draw a huge sigh of relief not having to keep on being the Savior of the human race! Without using God, Yahweh, Elohim, or Allah as a sword to wield power over others or impose his will on others, Buddha simply established ways of improving one's meditative powers to improve self and relations with others. His way of getting right with the world started with himself.

Here's a hypothetical and honest experiment to explore monotheistic religions, pagan beliefs, and atheist convictions. I would politely ask every believer and nonbeliever to accept the same faith for a month and record the results of how they understand morality, social injustice, and crime. For example, let the whole world turn Buddhist for a month and keep track of good and evil incidents for that month, and then turn to the next faith for a month and follow the same routine. I am confident that at the end of the experiment, the graph of good or evil would not show a surge either way for any religion. It doesn't matter which religion you choose, your God(s) is not making the world a better (or worse) place. Every month, the world would still be standing in the same spot—full of crimes, contradictions, and good and evil—that it is today. One potential positive outcome for the world would be that the entire human race wouldn't have to fear "rival" faiths anymore, as the whole world would have experienced the same faith at once. People would learn more about each other's faiths, which would hopefully dispel some misgivings that people have about each other and clear away all the bitterness that exists between religions. Chances are, however, that we human beings would still find a reason to disagree, quarrel, and even kill each other in the name of God.

# 23

## ONE GOD, VAST DIFFERENCES

Now let's look at the Qur'an's Surah 28:52–53: "Those to whom we sent the Book before this, they do believe in this revelation; if recited to them, they say: We believe in it, it is Truth from our Lord. Indeed, we have been Muslims bowing to God's will from this before." But bowing to God's will in and of itself does not qualify one as a Muslim. No record exists of a Muslim presence in the days of Noah, Abraham, Moses, and Jesus. The Old and New Testaments make no mention of Islam or Muhammad. According to Yusuf Ali, however, some early Christians and Jews not only welcomed and accepted Islam, but claimed that they had always been Muslims because they worshipped only one God.[76] In that sense, Adam, Noah, Abraham, Moses, and Jesus were all Muslims. And if Jesus was, in fact, a Muslim, shouldn't Catholic popes be considered Muslims too? Mahatma Gandhi, who occasionally quoted the Qur'an at his public conventions and political rallies, claimed to be a Muslim.[77]

Muslims can take their wishful thinking as far as they'd like, but Muhammad was the first Muslim, as he invented Islam. No evidence exists of the Islamic faith in the early life of Muhammad. It wasn't until the age of forty that Muhammad had his first religious revelation. So what beliefs did he have before then? The answer is that Muhammad would have shared the same pagan beliefs as his father, uncles, and close

---

[76] *Holy Qur'an*, 1,017.
[77] "Mahatma Gandhi Quotes," GoodReads.com, last modified 2014, https://www.goodreads.com/quotes/361107-yes-i-am-i-am-also-a-muslim-a-christian.

relatives. If Muslims existed prior to the establishment of Islam, God should have created only one holy book from day one. But it also would have contained man-made stories by self-proclaimed holy messengers and their disciples. The best thing God could have done would be to stop sending messenger after messenger, causing confusion, contradictions, and quarrels. Looking at God's holy water creek, I see that all His ducks did not line up in a row.

Another point of confusion in the Qur'an centers on Islamic attire for women. Surah 33:59 shows God instructing Muhammad on what to say to women about their manner of dress: "O Prophet! Tell thy wives and daughters, and the believing women, that they should cast their outer garments over their persons when abroad; it is convenient, they should know as such and not be molested." Surah 33:59 is the only verse in the whole Qur'an that addresses the issue of Islamic dress, and even then, it does not specify the face veil. A few other verses only vaguely touch on the subject of general attire. Surah 33:59 instructs women to wear an outer garment, but it does not define anything else, like measurements or the type of garment. Should it include a head scarf? How about *purdah, burqa, chador,* or *niqab* (face veils)? What parts of the body should be covered—just the bosom, or also the head, legs, arms, or hands, or even the eyes? Once again, the Qur'an claims to have an answer for all the moral codes of life, but it neglects to describe *hijab* (Islamic clothing) in any meaningful way. This issue is left in the hands of domineering Muslim clerics who have manipulated the vague Qur'anic description to their advantage for political, cultural, and moral reasons. However illiterate, unschooled, or immoral themselves, defenders of the faith, such as Taliban members in Afghanistan and police officers in Saudi Arabia, have the power to remind any female about Islamic attire by hitting her with a stick. If a woman forgets to cover her ankles, she can be physically assaulted and jailed as legal punishment. Where does the Qur'an discuss ankles or any kind of punishment regarding attire? Entrenched in their archaic notions of Islamic dress, these "defenders of the faith" cannot see or think with logic or reason; they resort to violence against women because of a religious matter that does not even appear in the Qur'an!

For Muslims, what to wear and how to cover depends largely on culture. The first recorded instance of veiling goes back roughly to the seventh century BC, in the Assyrian empire. Later, veiling became common in Mesopotamia and Greece, where it took the spotlight among society's elite class only. Currently in Saudi Arabia and the Gulf states, a woman's entire body must be covered except her hands and eyes. Other cultures require covering women's eyes, also, as in certain parts of Afghanistan. In some African cultures, wrapping the hair and covering the bosoms and legs signifies proper religious dress. A great variety of Islamic dress can be seen in the United States.

Let's just review a few facts at this point about two of the most prominent holy books. Many orthodox or fundamentalist Christians claim that the Bible is the literal "word of God," and therefore error-free. The Bible is a collection of sixty-six books, written by at least forty authors and compiled over a period of sixteen hundred years. Many claim that it inspires, motivates, and encourages people for the benefit of human life. But how did it become God's Word after having been written and rearranged by so many hands? When someone claims to "believe in the Bible," what on earth can they possibly mean? To "believe in the Bible" means to believe in so many outstanding contradictions and conflicting messages that one would have to have multiple personalities to handle the chaos!

The Qur'an contains roughly eighty thousand words, almost sixty-four hundred verses, and one hundred fourteen surahs. It plays a major role in everyday civil matters such as birth, death, and marriage. According to the Muslim faith, the Qur'an is the Mother of all Holy Books, and most Muslims believe that the Qur'an contains the "perfect words of God." According to Islam, the Qur'an is so unique that human hands could not have written it, and no other book like it has come before or after it. Surah 46:4 states, "Bring me a book Revealed before this, or any remnant of knowledge you may have, if you are telling the truth!" Here are some possible answers, actually. The Qur'an inadvertently answers the question in part, in Surah 53:36–37: "Nay, is he not acquainted with what is in the books of Moses and the book of Abraham who fulfilled his engagements?" The Qur'an acknowledges, then, that the Old Testament came before it. In addition, "the remnant of knowledge" could be considered as the

Pentateuch, the New Testament, the Code of Hammurabi, and the Hindu Gita, as well as Zoroaster's book on Arda Viraf.

Zoroaster was the founder of a religious philosophy of Greater Iran around sixth century BCE. He simplified the pantheon of early Iranian gods. It influenced other later religions including Judaism, Christianity, and Islam. The religious text is named "Arda Viraf." It describes the dream journey of devout Zoroaster through the next world.

Muslims claim that the Qur'an makes reference to knowledge that would have been unusual, if not miraculous, for anyone to have known in the time of the prophet Muhammad. Some Muslims claim that the Qur'an reveals knowledge of the existence of atoms and particles. I would simply like to know how and when the term *atom* sneaked into the Qur'an. Before Islamic and Greco-Roman civilizations, an Indian named Kanada originated the idea of the *anu* ("atom"). He was a Hindu sage who lived in either the second or sixth century BC; scholars dispute the time frame. Kanada believed that all living beings were composed of five elements: water, fire, earth, air, and ether. He believed that atoms were indestructible and therefore immortal.[78] The word *atom* is Greek in origin. The prefix *a* means "not" and *tomos* means "cut"—that is, literally, not able to be cut, indestructible. Kanada and the Greeks attempted to define the atom and explain its composition. Aristotle, however, strongly opposed the idea of the atom, and so it faded away until its reappearance in the theories of John Dolton, around 1808.

In Yusuf Ali's translation of the Qur'an, six surahs refer to the "weight of the smallest thing." The word for "weight" in Arabic is *masqala*, and the term for "the smallest thing" is *zarrah*. The Qur'an also uses *Zarrah* as a reference to "the tiniest thing, good or bad." (Usually that term has a moral meaning. According to Islam, on Judgment Day, each human being will find out every little good or bad thing he or she has ever said or done.) In Arabic, *Zarr* means "small ants" and refers to something tiny. The term for "atom" in Ali's translation, therefore, appears as *Masqala Zarrah*. In the Qur'an, the Arabic phrase *Masqala Zarrah* appears as a

[78] "Kanada," *Wikipedia*, last modified September 30, 2014, http://en.wikipedia.org/wiki/Kanada.

reference to issues of justice, in conjunction with the strength of God's character for being such a fair judge. The Qur'an does not explain the composition of *Masqala Zarrah* (atom) in any of the six verses that use that term. Those six verses are listed below, with emphasis added on the term that is translated in Arabic as *Masqala Zarrah*.[79]

+ Surah 4:40: "God is never unjust *in the least degree.*"
+ Surah 10:61: "Nor hidden from thy Lord so much as *the weight of an atom.*"
+ Surah 34:3: "From Him is not hidden the least little *atom* in Heavens or earth."
+ Surah 34:22: "Call on other gods, they have no power—not *the weight of an atom.*"
+ Surah 99: 7–8: "Then anyone who has done *an atom's weight* of good or an *atom's weight* of evil shall see it."

John Dolton uses the word *atom* in his theory as follows:

1. Everything is composed of atoms, which are indivisible building blocks of matter and cannot be destroyed.
2. All atoms of an element are identical.
3. The atoms of different elements differ in size and mass.
4. Compounds are produced through different whole-number combinations of atoms.
5. A chemical reaction results in the rearrangement of atoms in the reactant and product compounds.

Right or wrong, Dolton's theory provides a precise idea and understanding of an atom. Do the aforementioned six Qur'anic verses bear any resemblance to the ideas of Kanada, the Greek philosophers, or John Dolton? Not at all. This is because around the beginning of the twentieth century, the word *atom* began to be translated into Arabic as *Zarrah* for both lay and religious people. Thus, the word *Zarrah* acquired a *recent* meaning. The Qur'an did not originally use *Zarrah* to mean

---

[79] Ibid.

"atom."[80] This is a *new, modern* English translation. Throughout his translation of the Qur'an, Yusuf Ali consistently uses the term *Masqaal Zarrah* to mean "atom" except in one instance, in Surah 4:40, where it means "in the least degree." Multitudes of Muslim readers are simply ill-informed; they do not realize this was a new, recently added term (atom, modern English translation). The translators added one more voice to the false claim that the Qur'an mentions atoms, implying the existence of a miracle: Muhammad could only have known of atoms if Allah told him. If that were the case, then why did Muhammad not also know how big the earth was or the scientific conditions that produced thunder and lightning?

The angel Gabriel recited the Qur'an in Muhammad's native tongue of Arabic over a period of twenty-three years.[81] Muhammad could neither read nor write, so some of his companions wrote down the Qur'an, supposedly exactly as Muhammad dictated it. If this were a perfect work of God, why didn't God pick up a pen and write it? Again, with an undetermined (unproven) number of people writing the Qur'an, there is no way of tracking any changes to the text—an issue we will explore shortly.

Today, 15 percent of Muslims in the world speak Arabic.[82] The remaining 85 percent of non-Arabic-speaking Muslims often find themselves forced to learn the Qur'an in Arabic, particularly as children. Some of them memorize it without any clue as to what the words mean. After memorizing the Qur'an, innocent children get a pat on the back and the honorary title of *hafiz*. They then retain a respectable status in their community and mosque. They achieve an imaginary honor in the eternal world at the expense of memorizing the words of Allah in a foreign language.

Perhaps the facilitation of memorization explains the Qur'an's overwhelming propensity for repetition, and its rhyming nature (in

---

[80] Jochen Katz, "Does the Qur'an Speak About Atoms?," Answering Islam: A Christian-Muslim Dialogue, Answering-Islam.org, www.answering-islam.org/authors/katz/quran/science/atoms.html.

[81] "Beginning of Revelation," MissionIslam.com, http://www.missionislam.com/quran/beginrevelation.htm.

[82] "Arabic Language," Islam.About.com, last modified 2014, http://islam.about.com/od/arabiclanguage/.

Arabic). One other explanation might be poetic repetition. That is just an educated guess; otherwise it would be hard to explain the level of repetition in the Qur'an, which contains exactly matching verses, page after page. Surah 55:13, for example, repeats this verse thirty-one times, word for word: "Then which of the favors of your Lord will you deny?" Each verse describes a favor of the Lord to humans, and then repeats the question. We humans need not be reminded thirty-one times. Another example of extreme repetition occurs in the following verses:

+ Surah 53: 17, 22, 32, and 40: "And We have made this Qur'an easy to remember and understand."
+ Surah 54: 22, 32, and 40: "And We have made this Qur'an easy to remember and understand."
+ Surah 19:97: "And We have made this Qur'an easy in thine tongue."

Based on our earlier word count, more than half the Qur'an consists of repetitions! Without them, the Qur'an would amount to approximately two hundred pages. How can anyone assert that all the answers to human problems reside in two hundred pages?

Lack of clarity can also be seen in Surah 7:46: "Between them shall be a veil, and on the heights will be a man who would know everyone by his marks: they will call out to the companions of the garden ..." Does this verse make any sense at all to any average, intelligent human being? Let's turn to the expertise of Yusuf Ali for guidance. Ali comments, as he typically does, that "this is a difficult passage and commentators have interpreted it in different ways. The three distinct schools have their own version. The first school thinks the 'man on the Heights' is an angel. The second school holds him to be a soul, evenly balanced on the partition of Hell and Heaven. The third interpretation of the 'man on the Heights' resembles the first, with one exception: the partition and heights are figurative."[83] Do these distinct schools of thought clarify this image for us? Absolutely not. Like other wizards of religion, Ali relentlessly tries to link together various imaginative characters (the "man on the heights,"

---

[83] *Holy Qur'an*, 352.

souls, angels, and the companions of the garden), but it doesn't work. It's like building a sandcastle in the middle of a lake: anyone can imagine it, but nobody can build it. This complex, meaningless verse does not belong in the "easy to understand" Qur'an.

Here are some other observations that require further discussion:

1. If God can create anything with the simple command, "Be," why would it take Him six days to create heaven and earth? It took Gabriel twenty-three years to reveal the Qur'an's text, which was still incomplete at the time of Muhammad's death in AD 632. God should have known the time of Muhammad's death and planned better. Why did God leave it to Muhammad's followers to compile his recitations into a single book? By doing so, God started a lot of controversy regarding the origin of the Qur'an. Wouldn't it have been more convincing just to download the entire Qur'an in one sitting?

2. Abu-Bakr started the job of compiling the recitations of Muhammad, while Ali bin Abu Talib compiled his own version. In the time of the third caliph, Uthman, disagreements erupted regarding these two different versions of the Qur'an. Finally, Uthman, with the help of Hafsa, the daughter of Omar, ordered the preparation of an official text of the Qur'an. It remains today as the definitive text. The remaining contradictory versions were destroyed, but the controversies continued among early Muslims regarding the divine origin of the Qur'an.

3. After Muhammad's death, no one point of contact existed to collect his revelations. Many academics and followers of Muhammad tried to gather all the collections and make them one book. The first difficulty they encountered was that the text had no "points" (proper Arabic diacritical marks). Depending on where one puts the point on *h*, *j*, or *kh*, for example, the text can have different meanings. In AD 935, Ibn-Muja-Hid directed the creation of a set of rules for vowels and consonants in the Arabic language. This means that nearly three years passed between the

time Abu-Bakr and Ali bin Abu Talib began their versions and the time a clear, Arabic interpretive code was created.

4.  Surah 18:83 reads as follows: "They ask thee concerning Zul-Qarnain, say, 'I will rehearse to you something of a story.'" So who is Zul-Qarnain? Yusuf Ali tells us that the name *Zul-Qarnain* literally means "the two horned ones" or "the King with two horns."[84] Popular opinion identifies him as Alexander the Great. Alternative suggestions are that he was an ancient Persian or prehistoric Himyaritic king. No one seems to know—or the reference just can't be explained. We run into the same problem with Surah 18:56: "So they found one of Our servants, on whom we had bestowed mercy from Ourselves and whom We had taught knowledge from Our own presence." Again, Yusuf Ali offers an answer, saying that the servant's name is not mentioned in the Qur'an, but tradition gives the name as Khadir, gathered from a sum of picturesque folktales.[85] If Islamic religious scholars have trouble explaining these two characters, Zul-Qarnain and Khadir, how does an ordinary human stand to figure it out? And yet we're supposed to believe that the Qur'an is "easy to remember and understand," and that it contains "the perfect words of God."

5.  Why did Caliph Uthman have to put in order the text that existed at the time of Muhammad's death? God and Gabriel were supposed to provide guidance for the final chapter of the Qur'an. Why leave it to Uthman, Ali, Hafsa, Abu-Bakr, and Aisha? They compiled and standardized the Qur'an, leaving open the burning question, Did they arrange it according to their own political or personal agendas? What was the reason for rejecting Uthman's version? Most Muslims will tell you unequivocally that not one jot of the Qur'an has ever changed. That depends, however, on which time frame we consider. Which is the "real" Qur'an—the one that existed at the time of Muhammad's death

---

[84] *Holy Qur'an*, 753.
[85] Ibid., 748.

or the one compiled by Uthman into one book (or one of the many translations)? Some critics believe that Uthman omitted 25 percent of the original verses for political reasons![86] Also, Imam Ali's version of the Qur'an contains verses that are not seen in the Uthmanic Qur'an used today.

6. The first four Islamic caliphs—Abu-Bakr, Umar, Uthman, and Ali bin Abu Talib—ruled from 632 to 661 CE. The Google definition of the term *caliph* is "the chief Muslim civil and religious ruler, regarded as the successor of Muhammad." Their daughters' marriages linked the caliphs together. These daughters sometimes made open offers to become wives of Muhammad. As best as can be determined, Muhammad married between eleven and thirteen times during his lifetime, and the women varied in age, religion, and background. One of his wives was Abu-Bakr's daughter, Aisha. Muhammad also married Omar's daughter, Hafsa, when she was widowed at age eighteen. Omar first asked Uthman and Abu-Bakr if they would like to marry Hafsa, unaware that Muhammad had already expressed interest in her. Going against the boss (Muhammad) would have been a bad idea, so both Uthman and Abu-Bakr declined Omar's offer. When Omar went to Muhammad to complain about their refusal, Muhammad is reported to have said, "Hafsa will marry better than Uthman and Uthman will marry better than Hafsa"[87]—thus defusing the matter. Everyone left the situation happy winners. Uthman ended up marrying Muhammad's daughter Ruqayya, and following her death, he married Muhammad's other daughter, Kulthum. Ali was married to Muhammad's youngest daughter, Fatima. This intense closeness or interrelatedness among the caliphs was a strategic move designed to solidify the Islamic power structure.

---

[86] Time Warner Cable, "Facts on Islam, Chapter 16,"http://home.insightbb. com/~cathiadenham2/Facts%20on%20Islam/Islam%20%20-%20%2016.htm.

[87] "Hafsa bint Omar bin al-Khattab," IslamWeb.net, last modified June 21, 2003, http://www.islamweb.net/ehajj/printarticle.php?id=40070&lang=E.

7. Here are a few opening lines of the Qur'an, found in Surah 1:1–5, known as "The Fatiha":

Praise to God, The cherisher and sustainer of the worlds;
Most gracious, most merciful;
Master of the Day of Judgment
You do we worship and Thine aid we seek
Show us the straight path …

Surely these words didn't come from God. If they had, they would read as follows: "I, God, will show you the straight path." Rather, the Fatiha mimics the opening introduction at a political rally, complete with fanfare and pomp, before the main speaker takes central stage.

8. The number of days it took God to create heaven and earth varies greatly from surah to surah, as we see below:

* Surah 7:54 – 6 days
* Surah 41:9 – 2 days
* Surah 41:10 – 4 days
* Surah 41:12 – 2 days

Here are Yusuf Ali's explanations regarding the above surahs, respectively:

* "The creation in 6 days is of course metaphorical."[88]
* "This is a difficult passage, describing the primal creation of our physical Heavens around us."[89]
* "If we count 2 days in 41:9, 4 days in 41:10 and 2 days in 41:12; we get total of 8 days, while in many passages the creation is 6 days. The Commentators understand the 4 days in verse 10 and

---

[88] Ibid., 355.
[89] Ibid., 1,288.

2 days in verse 9, so the total the universe comes to 6 days. This is reasonable because verse 9 and 10 form really one series."[90]

Also, in his interpretation of Surah 70:4, Ali explains that a day in Qur'anic time means fifty thousand years in human time: "In a day measured whereof is fifty thousand years."[91] Likewise, he says, Surah 22:47 refers to a "day" as one thousand years.[92] Whoever wrote the Qur'an should have taken a more comprehensive look at the math regarding the number of days and years! Muhammad was not a learned or literate man by his own admission. If Muhammad did the calculating, then this proves that he was poor in math skills. Maybe he lost count of the days while reciting the Qur'an from Gabriel.

Muhammad isn't the only one with a bad sense of numbers. Hadith 21257, narrated by Ibn-Hanbal, asserts that the total number of holy messengers since Adam is 124,000. The Bible also reports this number. How Ibn-Hanbal manages to arrive at this figure remains a mystery; the numbers simply don't compute. Let's take a look at the math: The time span from Adam to Jesus was four thousand years. Six hundred more years passed from Jesus to Muhammad. A total of forty-six hundred years, then, passed from the first to the last holy messenger. If we assume an average age of eighty-five per prophet, then only fifty-four holy messengers have existed. How did the figure 124,000 come about?

Let's work another equation, looking at the age of the earth based on the assumption that there were 124,000 holy messengers (again, with an average age of eighty-five per messenger). This would mean that the earth is 10,540,000 years old. If we take into consideration the forty-six hundred years between Adam and Muhammad, then the average age of each messenger would be 13.4 days! It doesn't matter how we try to balance this equation, there's always one factor way out of proportion.

Here's yet another example of numbers gone awry: Genesis 16:16 tells us that Abraham was eight-six years old when Hagar bore him Ishmael. Abraham was ninety-nine years old when circumcised, and

---

[90] Ibid., 1,605.
[91] Ibid., 864.
[92] Ibid., 1,092.

Genesis 17:25 states that "his son Ishmael was thirteen years old when circumcised in the flesh of his foreskin." However, Genesis does not make clear Ishmael's age when Sarah sent him and his mother, Hagar, away. Apparently, Sarah got upset when she saw Isaac and Ishmael playing together. Ishmael was fourteen years older than Isaac. We have to assume that Isaac was at least three years old to have been able to move around and play with his older brother, who would have been seventeen at that point. Sarah told Abraham to cast out Hagar and Ishmael so that they wouldn't be able to inherit anything that she felt rightfully belonged to Isaac. Abraham went ahead and followed Sarah's orders. He got up early in the morning, gave bread and water to Hagar, and sent her out into the wilderness of Beer-Sheba. Oddly, the scriptures depict Ishmael, whom we know was at least seventeen years old, as a little baby. Genesis 21:15 states, "When the water was gone, she cast the child under one of the bushes." A boy of seventeen would have been strong and old enough to take care of his mother. It seems somehow that the author(s) of Genesis didn't think these stories through properly. If we assume that Ishmael was two or three years old at the time he and his mother were cast out, then Isaac would not have been born yet; in fact, he would have been minus twelve years old! Just as strange and puzzling is the following piece of information from Genesis 21:5: "Abraham was one hundred years old when his son Isaac was born to him."

Yet another example of numbers not adding up occurs in the story of Noah's Ark. In Genesis 6:15, God gives Noah exact instructions on how to make the ark, with a "length of 300 cubits [450 feet], width 50 cubits feet [75 feet], and height 30 cubits [45 feet] …" Noah did as he was told. The dimensions of Noah's Ark are not large by today's ship standards. It would have been a mission impossible to keep hundreds of thousands of animal pairs in a ship 450 feet by 75 feet by 45 feet for forty days. Animals cannot survive on human love. They need proper food as well as barriers to separate them. Let's consider an average zoo and consider if the animals in it could possibly live on Noah's boat. The Houston Zoo in Texas, for example, contains six thousand animals on fifty-five acres. This provides a relatively comfortable space of 400 square foot per animal. With six thousand animals (three thousand pairs), Noah's Ark provided 12.9 square feet of room for each animal, not including storage space for food and living space for Noah and his family.

9. If the Bible and the Qur'an are both "the word of God," why don't they contain the same information? For example, Genesis 12:10 describes Abraham's visit to Egypt, but the Qur'an contains no reference to it. Also, Genesis 25:2 discusses the "three wives of Abraham, Sarah, Hagar, and Keturah …"; according to the Bible, Abraham took a third wife named Keturah, who bore him six sons. The Qur'an does not mention this third wife or her sons.

10. Surah 2:125 states, "And remember Abraham and Ishmael raised the foundation of the house with this prayer: Our Lord! Accept this prayer from us, for you are the All-hearing, the All-knowing." The Bible, however, gives no evidence that Abraham and Ishmael were heading to Mecca to raise the foundation of the house.

First, Abraham migrated from his childhood hometown, Ur, to Haran, and then later he migrated to Egypt. In biblical times, Egypt represented "the American dream" of today. It was a rich and strong place with plenty of food located along the Nile coast. These conditions attracted thousands of people from neighboring countries who were in search of food and jobs. Abraham carried out the duties assigned to him by God; lived in the wilderness of Shur, Bear-Sheba, and Mamre; and died east of Mamre. Second, why would Abraham migrate again and travel seven hundred miles to Mecca to build the House of the Lord in Arabia? It was a country of poor and illiterate Bedouins, with no trace of water for hundreds of miles. Third, let's assume that Abraham did go to Mecca and build the House of the Lord. What happened, then, to the early so-called Muslims who followed Abraham and Ishmael? Did they just disappear? There is no evidence of Islam until Muhammad's appearance in the late sixth century. Abraham was buried east of Mamre, not in Mecca. This fact clearly shows that Abraham would have left Mecca without finishing his mission and gone back to his original settlement, close to Jerusalem. Contrary to Abraham, Muhammad did a bang-up job of spreading Allah's word and teaching Islam. He scored an A-plus in this department, with his mighty sword and intellectual ingenuity. After nearly fourteen hundred years, Muhammad's message is holding firm, well-founded, and steady.

In the early days of Islam, a huge rift existed between Jews and Muslims. Muhammad cleverly adopted a few Jewish traditions and customs, probably as a means of establishing some rapport with the Jews and recognition of his own religion. In the beginning of his teaching career, he tried to show strong similarities between himself and Moses in terms of their common message. That didn't sit well with the Jews, so like any shrewd leader, he tried a new game plan: he took his newborn philosophy of Islam, bypassed Moses and Jesus, and affixed it firmly to Abraham. After twenty-five hundred years, there were no followers of Abraham to refute Muhammad's teachings. Few people at the time really had a clue about Abraham until Muhammad propagated the idea of the monotheistic religions. In this way, Muhammad could establish a respectable foundation for his own religion, as Surah 3:67 asserts: "Abraham was not a Jew, nor Christian, but was true in faith and bowed his will to God which is Islam." If Abraham had in fact been a true Muslim, this surah would have stated the following: "Abraham was not a Jew, nor Christian, but a true Muslim." Such a statement would affirm the notion that bowing to the will of God makes one a Muslim.

Many followers of each monotheistic faith tend to have fixed and rigid beliefs, and they either don't know or decline to accept facts that contradict their beliefs. Many would be shocked to learn that their religions' stories of great floods and the creation of the world originated thousands of years ago as old myths and legends from different cultures. After several mutations, these same stories were subsumed by the monotheistic religions, complete with such characters as El, Elohim, Yahweh, God, Allah, and Jesus. Some myths and characters cross over between the pagan and Muslim faiths, despite the great discrepancies between them.

# 24

## PAGAN AND MONOTHEISTIC GODS: DIFFERENT YET SIMILAR

According to Hindu belief, the deities Vishnu and Lakshmi rode on the back of a large, humanoid bird named Garuda[93] to reach heaven, known in Hindi as Vaikuntha. This may call to mind Muhammad's Night Journey, when he went to heaven on a winged horse and met many prophets including Abraham, Moses, and Jesus, and ultimately Gabriel took Muhammad into paradise to meet God. Stories of similar mythical journeys abound throughout religious history. According to Zoroastrian pagan literature, Arda Viraf[94] went to heaven to find out what was happening there. He climbed to the third heaven and met the angels and the heavenly chiefs, just as Muhammad did. Arda Viraf came back to earth to tell his people what he had seen. Vishnu rode on Garuda, Muhammad rode on Buraq, and poor Arda Viraf presumably had to walk. They all made it to heaven anyway and came back with similar stories. These stories serve as yet another example of how the holy messengers conveniently copied or borrowed myths from other religions in order to gain their own dramatic firepower. They also may have been looking for credibility by reworking prior stories; if people can connect to a story through the memory of a similar story, they might feel more

---

[93] "Garuda," *Wikipedia*, last modified October 7, 2014, http://en.wikipedia.org/wiki/Garuda.

[94] "Arda Viraf," *Wikipedia*, last modified June 3, 2014, http://en.wikipedia.org/wiki/Book_of_Arda_Viraf.

inclined to trust the "new" story. This similarity can also work against credibility, of course, signifying that the new is just a rehash of the old. Of course, to some degree, we have to cut the holy messengers some slack. They had a hard sell trying to make belief in God appealing. They had to convince people of the "truth" about God while also presenting Him as a typical commander in chief.

Let's compare another mythical story, that of the Twelve Labors of Hercules, with the story of Muhammad's Night Journey and ascension to heaven. It seems that Hercules had an anger management problem of the worst kind. In today's parlance, he was the most dangerous kind of domestic abuser. According to the Greek myth, Hercules killed his wife and three children in a fit of rage. The king ordered him to perform certain impossible missions as penance, such as removing the skin of a lion who cannot be pierced or wounded by any kind of weapon; killing a multiheaded serpent that grows new heads when one of its own is removed; and driving off enormous birds that possess dangerous, knifelike feathers that fall from the sky like daggers. This sounds like a captivating, mind-boggling story fit for the Hollywood screen, even by today's standards. Hercules did succeed in each of his impossible tasks.[95] It is no wonder the Greeks loved him—not only for his mighty strength, but because of his fearless determination never to quit.

The thrilling nature of Hercules's conquests notwithstanding, several questions arise in response to this bizarre myth:

1. Who was this brainless king who assigned Hercules to find a special lion, a special serpent, and birds with feathers that fell like knives? The point is that these creatures never existed. If a creature does not exist, how is someone going to find it? But Hercules did. Hercules succeeded in all twelve labors and became a hero.
2. Who recorded the details of his accomplishments?

---

[95] "Labours of Hercules," *Wikipedia*, last modified October 9, 2014, http://en.wikipedia.org/wiki/Labours_of_Hercules.

3.  How long did it take Hercules to complete each of these impossible missions?

No answers to these questions exist anywhere, but the stories capture the reader's imagination, even today. The same holds true for stories from the Bible and the Qur'an. Having heard them enough times, people everywhere began to recognize them until they became popular. They then became firmly installed in common memory. People don't ask questions about the absurd stories of Hercules; they simply accept him as a heroic, mighty figure. The same process applies to religious stories. It doesn't matter how far-fetched they sound; once fixed in the brain, they live forever.

Now let's take a more in-depth look at the fantastical story of Muhammad's Night Journey, also known as the Miraj, told partly in the Qur'an and partly in the Hadiths. It starts out as a simple, unpretentious story. Surah 17:1 relates it this way: "Glory to God who did take His servant for a journey by night from the Sacred Mosque to the farthest mosque, in order that We might show him some of our signs." But the Night Journey turns out to be a captivating, although illogical, story taken down in writing by the authors of the Hadiths, ostensibly in accordance with Muhammad's original recitation of events. Whether Muhammad went on this journey physically or spiritually is a matter of debate. If God had taken Muhammad on a trip to heaven, He would have added more to the Qur'an than just Surah 17:1, embellishing it with more significant details. As usual, however, the human writers of the Hadiths stretched the story to their liking and to fit their overall agenda: to garner huge interest in the prophet Muhammad.

Here is a section of the Night Journey as narrated by Anas bin Malik:

> Gabriel took charge of Muhammad before climbing to Heaven. Gabriel cut him open from throat to chest and took out all the material from his chest and abdomen. He washed them with ZamZam water with his own hands until he cleaned the inside of his body. Then a gold tray containing a gold bowl full of belief and wisdom was

brought to him. Gabriel stuffed his chest and throat with blood vessels and closed his chest. He then climbed with him to Heaven.[96]

What a gruesome scene! What bizarre and disturbing imagery! That does not sound like a narration by Muhammad after his biggest ordeal with Allah. In Surah 18:110, Muhammad says, "I am a man like yourselves," yet he sounds more like some kind of alien creature here. How does this quasi-surgical procedure by an angel make him a regular Joe? Did Muhammad have to go through another surgery before landing back on earth to keep his human form? Presumably, Gabriel put everything back in place; perhaps that was too gruesome an event for the writers to convey.

At any rate, a wife knows best regarding the physical state of her husband at night. In the Hadith, Muhammad's wife Aisha is reported to have said that his body remained within her sight during the Night Journey. This must mean that God took his spirit travelling. The Bible and the Qur'an are both jam-packed with stories about spirit journeys, visions, dreams, revelations, prophecies, and miracles at every turn. About the Night Journey, Muhammad said, "My eye was sleeping but my heart was awake." How does that happen? Why did God have to put Muhammad in an abnormal trance state for Muhammad to meet Him? It seems the impossible only happens to holy messengers and Hercules.

---

[96] "Hadith #1," IslamiCity.com, last modified October 9, 2014, http://www.islamicity.com/mosque/isra/israa_Miraj_Hadith.shtml.

# 25

## CATHOLIC POPES AND SAINTS

Sometimes the impossible happens the other way around though; the ones we should least expect to display bizarre behavior are the ones who do, such as popes. The papacy remains a visible and orderly link created by human beings between the throne of a human and the throne of God. Every pope is a human being first and last. His birth and death occur just like any other human's. He also has a character like any human—tainted with mistakes and common failings such as pride, a lust for power, jealousy, poor judgment, and so on. Peter[97] was the first self-proclaimed pope, with his own faults and accountabilities as well, as listed below:

1. After Jesus was arrested, Peter joined the other disciples in promptly hightailing it out of town. Rather than publicly claim his association with Jesus, he hid from the law so as not to meet a fate similar to that of his Lord.

2. All four Gospels recount the story of Peter chopping the ear off a high priest when Jesus was arrested. What a humble, God-fearing, and loving pope! Is chopping ears off a prerequisite for the papacy? Did Peter have other such saintly credentials?

3. With the blessing of Jesus, Peter presided as the Christian leader for seven years, after which time he went to Rome and promptly

---

[97] "Peter and Rome," CogWriter.com, last modified 2014, http://www.cogwriter.com/peter.htm.

overthrew Simon Magus. Magus[98] was a religious figure who had turned to Christianity and been baptized by Philip the Evangelist, but who was really more of a pagan and a magician. Having conquered Magus's throne, as it were, Peter held on to that priestly chair for twenty-five years.

4. Peter himself set up a senate for the Roman Church consisting of twenty-four priests and deacons. Who gave him the authority to create a senate for the Roman Church? Did he receive a divine message from God? Or did he just enjoy management a great deal?

5. Saint Peter had a highly stormy association with Saint Paul. It seems Peter thrived on conflict.

Peter was the first pope of Rome but certainly not the worst. Out of the holy chain of 266 popes, some were stripped of their titles due to bad behavior, some underwent criminal investigations, and some even served jail time. Ten, in particular, share the "Worst Pope Award" in Catholic history: Alexander VI, John XII, Benedict IX, Sergius III, Stephen VI, Julius III, Urban II, Clement VI, Leo X, and Boniface VIII.[99] Their records are full of accounts of lewd sexual acts followed by cover-ups through which they paid off their wrongdoings. Churches funded lavish parties. Pope John XII (935–64) turned the papal palace into a violent whorehouse, quite literally, in which men were mutilated and a deceased pope's corpse was even dug up for trial. Some might argue that ten is an insignificant number of naughty popes—but those were just the worst ones. We should expect any person who holds such a high office, and who communes directly with God, to be accountable to a higher moral standard. The number of naughty popes should be zero. Where was God, who supposedly oversees every minute of human behavior? God missed an opportunity to save face by chastising these corrupt and immoral popes, as well as kings and His own holy messengers, who falsely claimed for thousands of years to embody a divine link to Him.

---

[98] "Simon Peter versus Simon the Sorcerer or St. Peter Meets the Competition!!," Reformation.org, www.reformation.org/simon_peter_versus_simon_magus.html.
[99] http://www.toptenz.net/top-10-worst-popes-in-history.php

Abuse of office still exists today inside the secret walls of the Catholic Church. Certain media enterprises, such as Butler Television, do their best to dig up and expose the bad behavior of church officials to the rest of world. It is a sobering thought that believers in the faith put such blind trust in their leaders and live in such denial. This same blind faith registered on believers' faces in February 2013, as they listened to Pope Benedict's farewell address. Benedict looked down from the papal balcony upon a sea of teary people awaiting his blessing. Didn't any of them think about the horror of child sexual molestation, money laundering, and other crimes related to the power struggle that occurred during holy Benedict's eight-year reign?[100] Here is a brief account of Benedict's professional history:

As a child, he was a member of the Hitler Youth.[101] Although people protest that he was only a child at the time, the fact remains that he must have been affected deeply by this kind of early brainwashing. His parents presumably enrolled him in this Nazi endeavor, so he was well-indoctrinated into Nazi philosophy before and after his shameful stint in the Hitler Youth. After being ordained a priest, he became a university theologian. In 1977, Pope Paul VI appointed him as a cardinal and the Archbishop of Munich. In 1981, he became prelate of the Congregation of the Doctrine of Faith. He was the most respected, influential, and controversial member of the College of Cardinals, and he was the closest confidant of Pope John Paul II. To achieve the papal throne, Benedict followed the "correct" theological path, except when it came to decisive, active, and charismatic leadership. He woefully lacked these skills and seemed to be missing a sense of moral compunction. When the wicked crime of child sexual abuse was brought to his official attention when he was a cardinal, he merely turned his face while giving lip service to the

---

[100] Lizzie Davis, "Vatican Prelate Accused of Money Laundering," TheGuardian. com, last modified January 21, 2014, http://www.theguardian.com/world/2014/ jan/21/vatican-priest-accused-money-laundering.

[101] Susan Donaldson James, "Pope Benedict Dogged by Hitler Youth Past, Despite Jewish Support," ABCNews.com, last modified February 12, 2013, http://abcnews.go.com/International/ pope-benedict-dogged-nazi-past-achievements-jewish-relations/story?id=18469350.

issue. He ordered no investigation of the priests allegedly involved. As pope, he decreed that the sexual abuse of minors would be handled by his congregation, and the details of such cases were considered "papal secrets," much like the contents of confessions. During his emotional farewell speech, the pope admitted that "it sometime felt as if God was asleep during the troubled days of my papacy."[102] It is inconceivable that he tried to blame God for falling asleep at the wheel! Benedict's statement is a perfect reflection of how popes, holy messengers, and disciples of faith have created the image of God themselves to suit their convenience. Here is another mind-boggling statement by Pope Benedict XVI to Irish Catholics: "It is a *mystery* why Priests and other church officials abused children entrusted in their care" (emphasis added).[103]

In the 1970s, a theory surfaced about pedophilia that suggested that man-boy (adult-child) sexual liaisons were somehow wholesome and "normal." As a highly disturbing response to this theory, Catholic theologians argued that, in and of itself, pedophilia was neither evil nor good.[104] It is alarming that religious academics, spiritual leaders, and even the highest officials of the Catholic Church could make such a damaging statement. In addition, there is nothing "mysterious" about the sexual abuse of children by priests and church officials. Sexual abuse is an atrocious crime. It happens because pedophiles take advantage of their social status to ingratiate themselves to families where young children are available. Parents trust their religious leaders with their children. How the abuse of children by priests could strike some church officials as a mystery is almost beyond belief. Like many others, Pope Benedict XVI turned a blind eye to this horrendous crime against children. He

[102] Nick Squires, "Pope's Final Address: God Was Asleep on My Watch," Telegraph.co.uk, last modified February 27, 2013, http://www.telegraph.co.uk/news/religion/the-pope/9896792/Popes-final-address-God-was-asleep-on-my-watch.html.
[103] Frances D'Emilio, Associated Press, "Pope to Irish: Child Abuse by Clergy a 'Mystery,'" Boston.com, last modified June 17, 2012, http://www.boston.com/news/world/europe/articles/2012/06/17/pope_to_irish__child_abuse_by_clergy_shook__faith/.
[104] "On the Crisis, Does the Pope Have It Right?" NCROnline.org, last modified December 20, 2010, ncronline.org/blogs/ncr-today/crisis-does-pope-have-it-right.

swept allegations of abuse under the rug and then denied knowledge of them. That is not a defense; it's part of the problem.

The average age of a Vatican cardinal is seventy-eight, and the number of Catholics in their thirties is around half a billion. This puts a wide age gap between the cardinals and a great many Catholics. These seventy-eight-year-old cardinals need to break generational barriers and orient themselves more toward the lives and concerns of younger Catholics. Indeed, the Holy Church needs to consider putting in place some common-sense reformations. Some key suggestions follow:

1. Bring the average age of cardinals down to a maximum of fifty-eight.
2. The pope himself should have to submit to a series of checks and balances, as opposed to being able to make important decisions single-handedly.
3. He and all other priests should have to submit periodically to a child abuse background check.
4. Transparency needs to come to the forefront, making "behind closed doors" deals obsolete. If nothing is hidden from the sight of God, then the pope (who represents God on earth) should not be able to hide his deeds and misdeeds.

Religion in general, Bible stories, and priests, in particular, are supposed to teach us how to live in a more honest and meaningful way. The great irony here is that somehow this point eludes those who should know best how to live a moral life.

In the Catholic tradition, saints are the ones people look to for the ultimate in exemplary behavior. The Roman Catholic Church acknowledges saints the way some people regard "superhumans." The Google definition of a saint is "a person acknowledged as holy or virtuous and typically regarded as being in heaven after death." Saints don't achieve immediate acceptance into heaven easily, however. Catholics regard saints as exceedingly noble human beings who display unusually remarkable or heroic religious devotion, often made visible by the performance of miracles or some other obvious, God-assisted abilities. Nine times out of ten, they maintain loyalty to God in the face of extreme oppression. When Catholics pray to a particular saint, they typically seek the benefit of a blessing or ability that only he or she can provide. Saint Anthony, for example, is the official saint of lost items. If you lose your keys, you have him to thank should you find them.

No scriptural evidence for sainthood exists in any of the holy books. The whole notion of saints is yet another human conception, starting with God Himself. When people achieve sainthood, they are already dead. This makes sense, because dead people can't explain or demonstrate their particular prized ability—bleeding tears, exhibiting the sign of the stigmata on their hands, enduring fire unscathed, or whatever their amazing skill might be. When someone goes the extra mile serving humanity, there is no harm in honoring that person with, say, a title, plaque, prize, or cash reward. But with sainthood, what should have remained simple admiration for heightened bravery or kindness becomes, in the human imagination, stretched beyond the limits of believability. Sainthood is an artificial concept courtesy of slightly sneaky "holy men" earlier in history. Most likely, the creators of sainthood hoped to boost their religion among the masses. What a great draw, to claim you have a saint on your team! It's almost like having an invisible freak show at your disposal, and human beings always take an interest in the bizarre. But does God need this kind of unusual recognition, or could He be annoyed at the potential rivalry? (After all, the saints displayed their outstanding faith in some ways that were far more entertaining than God.) We can only wonder.

Even more exciting is the unspoken understanding that all current cardinals, and the pope himself, are on an invisible waiting list for sainthood. Interestingly, in 1983, Pope John Paul II changed the set of credentials necessary to become a saint. We don't know if this new copy of Standard Saint Operating Procedures ever reached the great hand of God, but apparently God needed an update. Currently, there are three progressive steps to sainthood:

1. You become one of the venerable. This means the Vatican has put you under investigation to determine just how virtuous a life you lived here on earth. At this point, you are dead.

2. You reach beatification. The pope formally declares you, a venerably deceased person, "blessed." As a beatified person, you are now assumed to be in heaven, enjoying special status.

3. You made it to canonization! This is the final step that confirms that, yes, you are indeed in heaven, enjoying your special status as we speak.

How exactly does the Vatican find out whether you made it to heaven? They must use some sort of spiritual background check. That raises the next question: What gives the Vatican the authority to make this determination?

# 26

## THE BHAGAVAD GITA

Another holy book designed to inspire people to behave their very best is the Bhagavad Gita, the Hindu equivalent of the Bible. These literary and philosophical scriptures emerged somewhere between 400 BC and AD 200. Although its authorship is not entirely clear, the Bhagavad Gita is said to have been written primarily by a man named Vyasa, whose identity also is not clear.[105] Known simply as the Gita, it contains eighteen chapters, and its verses affirm that God is the eternal force behind the universe. Its spiritual messages are said to touch on all phases of life. The following chapter descriptions provide a brief idea of the subject matter covered in the Gita:[106]

> Chapter 8: This chapter reveals much about the difference between the spiritual and material worlds and the afterlife—in particular, the light and dark paths a soul can take after death.
>
> Chapter 14: This chapter discusses the nature of goodness, passion, and ignorance, and their influence on living entities.
>
> Chapter 15: Krishna describes the transcendental character of God as omnipotent, omniscient, and omnipresent. He

---

[105] "Bhagavad Gita," *Wikipedia*, last modified October 6, 2014, http://en.wikipedia.org/wiki/Bhagavad_Gita.
[106] Ibid.

describes a symbolic tree representing material existence— its roots in heaven and foliage on earth.

Chapter 16: We learn in this chapter that in order to earn a supreme destination, we must abandon the forces of lust, anger, and greed that separate right from wrong.

Chapter 17: Krishna discusses the three separations of faith, thoughts and deeds, and eating habits.

Chapter 18: This section reviews the previous seventeen chapters. Krishna asks Arjuna to abandon all forms of attachment to the world and surrender to him, and he describes this surrender as perfecting life.

The eighteen chapters of the Gita tell a chronological story as Krishna (a supreme deity) leads Arjuna (representing humanity) up the divine ladder one rung at a time toward the final achievement of a perfect life. We can link the subject of each chapter mentioned above to the scriptures of monotheistic religions and observe several key similarities. Again, these similarities aren't random; rather, they confirm that monotheistic religions indeed have their scriptural roots firmly embedded in pagan mythology. To more clearly illuminate these scriptural similarities, let's take a look at one of them as it exists in the Bible, the Qur'an, and the Gita.

Surah 3:180 admonishes us to "let not those who greedily withhold of gifts which God has given them. Soon shall the things which they greedily withheld be tied to their necks on Judgment Day"—that is, focusing too much on the world's material wealth signifies a selfish soul who will be condemned. Likewise, John 2:15 cautions us, "Do not love the world or the things in this world." And we are all familiar with the popular adage found in Timothy 6:10: "For the love of money is the root cause of all evils." The Gita also implores humanity not to become overly embroiled in worldly matters; at one point, Krishna urges Arjuna to carry out his tasks "devoid of attachment, greed."[107]

Another similarity of content exists between chapter 16 of the Gita and certain parts of the Bible. The Gita 16:4 addresses the signs of evil in this way: "Arrogance, pride, anger, conceit, harshness and ignorance—these qualities belong to those of demoniac nature, O son of Prtha." Romans 12:17 also admonishes against evil, saying, "Repay no one evil with evil. Have regard for good things in the sight of all men." Ephesians 4:31 similarly echoes the Gita: "Let all bitterness, wrath, anger, clamor, evil speaking be put away from you, with all malice." The contents of all three verses sound very similar. In many respects, the only constant and obvious difference among them is the name of their God. But ask hard-core monotheistic believers about the pagan Gita, and the majority of them will either have no knowledge of it or reject it outright with extreme prejudice.

---

[107] Rajvir Singh, "Mystery of Soul and Life and Solutions to all Worldly Evils," *Why I Love Hinduism* (blog), June 5, 2014, http://vedicambassador.wordpress. com/2013/06/05/mystery- of-soul-and-life-and-solutions-to-all-worldly-evils/.

# 27

## GOD HAD NO CHOICE BUT TO GIVE FREE WILL TO HUMANS

A common theme that appears among holy scriptures is free will. Holy scriptures define good and evil (right and wrong) behaviors and relate at least some of their consequences. Human beings retain the right to choose how to behave. *Free will* can be defined as a choice between two or more alternatives, a choice made entirely of one's own accord. It has been a topic of furious debate, literally for ages. God gave human beings free will to experience love, happiness, and pleasure as well as hatred, misery, and discomfort. Given what humans often do with free will, it seems that God would have been wiser to present the choices of good, better, and best instead of good and evil only.

Surah 4:79 tells us, "Whatever good, O man happens to you, is from God; but whatever evil happens to you is from thy own soul." Doesn't this put us in a spiritual jam? What are we supposed to say to this—"Thanks a lot"? God gave humans only two alternatives, good and evil, by which to navigate this complex world. Some humans really do try to make the best use of free will. As usual, though, God gets to look better than we do; He gets to be good all the time while we struggle with good and evil. This provides yet another example of how God thinks and acts like a human—setting Himself up for a better scenario, even at the expense of others. If God was liberal enough to give us free will, He should have equipped us with the right tools to make a better life.

After God's outrageous experience with His closest partner, Satan,

He had almost no choice but to give free will to humans. Satan had shocked God enormously by saying no. Qur'an 2:34 states, "and behold, We said to the angels: 'Bow down to Adam:' and they bowed down: Not so Iblis (Satan): he refused and was haughty: he was those who reject Faith." This was an honest and free answer—not something to which God was accustomed. Once Satan rebelled, God knew that humans would no doubt provide an encore, regardless of His good guidance. He was wise this time and didn't lose sleep over the matter. It was to His *advantage* to grant humanity free will; by proactively addressing the inevitable human rebellion, God got to claim greatness for allowing humans to use their own judgment, while keeping the blame on them. God appears generous by offering free will to humans, but ultimately, He's still the titleholder of that free pass. What good is free will if it's attached to the lingering shadow of guilt? It's like having the Sword of Damocles hanging constantly overhead.[108]

---

[108] "Damocles," *Wikipedia*, last modified January 8, 2015, http://en.wikipedia.org/wiki/Damocles.

# 28

## THE IMPOSSIBILITIES OF TODAY ARE
## THE POSSIBILITIES OF TOMORROW

Until now, we've spent a lot of time discussing the historical (and imaginary) past. But what about today and even the future? Past impossibilities are the realities of today, and today's impossibilities are the realities of the future. Humans are constantly finding ways to make life easier. Turning for a moment back to myths and magic, let's look at "Ali Baba and the Forty Thieves," the popular children's story—part thriller and part fantasy. Although this story has been around a good while, it continues to speak to the reality of the changing times. Ali Baba has only one way to open or close the treasure box—with the magical phrases "Open Sim" and "Close Sim." This kind of "magical" ability exists in nearly every household today. You don't have to leave the comfort of your car in the rain and exert energy to open your garage door; you simply press a button, and voila! The garage door opens in a few seconds with just the touch of a finger.

Likewise, in the past, when people saw a tremendous storm approaching, they would pick up a rosary (or some similar item) and begin to recite various prayers to God, hoping for survival. They had no other means or knowledge available at the time to cope with an impending threat. Their only recourse was to look up to the sky and beg for God's mercy. Reciting prayers does not provide any guidance for escaping a storm. Today, cell phones, iPads, and iPhones have replaced the rosary; technology gives us instant information with which to make decisions in case of danger. Detailed forecasts and warnings regarding the intensity, speed, and direction of approaching storms prove mostly accurate these days, providing a more reliable way of saving lives than using lips and hands in prayer!

A common concept among most religions is that of life after death—a concept that has survived for thousands of years. As we discussed earlier, accepting death tends to be difficult for humans. The idea of continuing on into another life gives us hope and comfort. Understandably, we are afraid to die, and so a conception of life after death helps quell that fear. Someday this will be a common phrase: "life after life with no end in sight." As we go on increasing people's overall health and life span, we will eventually conquer death. We won't hear about it tomorrow on *Good Morning America*, but it will happen in the next fifty thousand years or so, if humanity lasts that long. Once we conquer the specter of death, the concept of God will become ancient history, relegated to museums to collect dust. Here are a few more impossibilities of today that could become tomorrow's possibilities:

+ We are concerned about the rising global population, which will continue to cause food shortages. In the next fifty thousand years, we may well invent a pill as a substitute for meals.
+ This change in nutritional intake will also help solve the housing shortage. To make enough room on earth for everybody, the human body size will eventually decrease from an average of five feet eight to much shorter. Obesity will become obsolete.
+ Today, newspapers and books are on the verge of disappearing; someday, computers, smart phones, and other high-tech gadgets will become obsolete too. It's only a matter of time. As technology advances toward the micro level, newborns will have chips implanted in their brains to store all the knowledge and skills gained from a typical education and work experience. These chips will enable kids to think, act, and behave like adults without having to go through the long hardship of childhood as well as fourteen to sixteen years of school and college education. These chips will contain all the latest available information

regarding the arts, science, and medicine; they may even facilitate mental telepathy. It may become impossible to prove that today's generation even existed.

Speaking of proof, Surah 28:75 of the Qur'an states, "And from each people shall we draw a witness, and we shall say: 'Produce your proof.'" Similarly, Surah 35:40 issues this challenge: "Show me what it is they have created in the wide earth? Or have they a share in the Heavens? Or have We given them a book from which they can derive clear evidence? The wrongdoers promise one another nothing but delusions." Thinking back to Abraham's humiliating rant against the pagans' stone idols, we could argue that the demand to "produce your proof" should have applied to both the pagans and monotheistic believers alike. But with Abraham, proof was a one-way street. He challenged the pagans most vociferously to produce proof that their gods actually existed in their stone shells. And yet Abraham, like God, was not prepared to do the same. His hard-core, fundamental stance based solely on "faith" had no link to logic or evidence. Holy messengers and religious academics struggled for centuries to prove the existence of God based on faith only. It is no wonder, then, that there's been a constant battle between nonbelievers and the faithful.

God's request for examples of human ingenuity seems somewhat absurd, coming from a God of supreme intelligence who knows all. Today, the proof of what humans have created on earth is actually substantial. So far, human beings have created many necessary essentials and comforts to improve their daily lives.

In the area of food production, we have greatly increased the total amount of food worldwide, and we have perfected the art of preserving food for transportation. We succeeded despite God's strategic positioning of various weather-related roadblocks, such as droughts, floods, and tornadoes.

Regarding building and architecture, we have created the tallest buildings ever through our own ingenious blend of art and science. We can honestly claim that we spent our money and time well to establish innovative buildings that have improved our communities. Here are three of our most magnificent creations:

1. Burj Khalifa in Dubai towers a whopping 2,713 feet tall, with 163 floors.
2. The Mecca Royal Clock Hotel in Saudi Arabia measures an impressive 1,971 feet, with 120 floors.
3. Taipei 101 in Taiwan stands 1,670 feet tall, with 101 floors.

Also, we have advanced impressively in the area of medical science. Once an unknown entity, cancer can now be arrested when detected early enough, and the medical profession continues to make gains even against persistent, aggressive forms of the disease. Through vaccinations, we have all but eliminated diseases that once threatened human life. These are just a few key examples; itemizing every enormous scientific advance would require an inordinate amount of time and thousands of pages.

# 29

## IS ISLAM A RELIGION OF PEACE?

We have reviewed the dangers of blind belief in an all-powerful, invisible God—such as brainwashing, the abuse of power, political subjugation of the masses, and child endangerment, to name a few. Other dangers also blatantly exceed the limits of acceptable behavior. We can't turn on the news today without seeing tremendous violence done in the name of God. Today, it seems that Islam suffers from multiple personalities; so many different sects, representing so many schools of thought, cause all kinds of excessive and un-Islamic behavior. The vast majority of Muslims who claim that Islam is a religion of peace serve as excellent examples of that argument. They live peacefully and don't cause disturbances. It's not the majority of Muslims who cause mayhem in the world. Most Muslims understand that the only circumstances under which they are permitted to use force against anyone is when their lives are directly and imminently threatened—and even then, the first resort is to engage in strategic negotiation. It's the few but growing number of Islamic extremists who distort Islam, making all Muslims look suspicious; you can't tell just by looking who's an extremist and who isn't.

To Islamic extremists, a threat doesn't have to be direct or imminent; to them, it's enough of a threat that America, "the Great Satan," exists, and in their minds it gives them license to attack. These people frequently take phrases from the Qur'an out of historical and theological context and use them to suit their current political purposes. One has to wonder if the religion itself truly means anything to these extremists—or whether they even adhere to any of the Five Pillars of Islam. Yet they are the ones ordering the rest of the world to "convert or die." (Converting others is not done in mainstream Islam!) To them, power over others is the main gain of religion. Without any compunction or reason, they declare that certain societies, people, or things are evil, and therefore a threat to Islam. Certain literary works, for example, pose a threat to Islam, in their eyes. Has any poem, book, or speech been used against Allah in such a way as to warrant a license to kill? A good example of using literature as a license to kill is the case of Asma Bint Marwan, a poet in the early days of Islam. She had no fondness for the faith, and her poetry incited pagans to become violent against Muhammad. She ended up paying the price for this with her life, while breast-feeding her babies.[109]

We find a more recent example in the case of writer Salman Rushdie, whose well-known book, *The Satanic Verses*, takes a satirical look at the life of the prophet Muhammad. The majority of Islamic extremists didn't even read the book; they readily accepted the Ayatollah Khomeini's *fatwa* (order) for Rushdie's execution. As a result, Salman Rushdie went into hiding for years, in fear for his life. According to Islamic extremists, Islam is only a religion of peace provided you agree with them. If you don't, they will kill you to preserve the "peace." Sadly, the survivors of the recent slaughter at the Paris headquarters of *Charlie Hebdo* know this all too well. Highly offended by the magazine's satirical cartoons of the prophet Muhammad, several radical Muslims believed they had the right to murder the artists and publishers of *Charlie Hebdo*.[110]

If taken out of historical context or to an extreme, any verse from any holy book can become justification for oppressive behavior, if not violence. Surah 2:7 states, "God set a seal on their hearts and on their hearing and on their eyes is a veil; great is the penalty they incur." What should serve as a reminder not to close our hearts and minds to God becomes, in extremists' minds, a fatwa against any and all rejecters

---

[109] "Asma bint Marwan," *Wikipedia*, last modified October 8, 2014, http://en.wikipedia.org/wiki/%27Asma%27_bint_Marwan.
[110] "Charlie Hebdo Attack: Helicopters Hunt for Suspects in Woods of France," CNN.com, last modified January 8, 2015, http://www.cnn.com/2015/01/08/europe/charlie-hebdo-paris-shooting/.

of Islam. The Qur'an includes many references to the punishment of nonbelievers. In the wrong minds and hands, and taken out of their specific, historical contexts, these verses become a license to bring great violence against others, Muslims and non-Muslims alike. This is also true of a phrase typically used only in *peaceful* circumstances to praise Allah: *Allahu Akbar,* or "God is great." Today, Islamic extremists shout this phrase, grotesquely enough, prior to committing acts of barbarism; the emotional cry "Allahu Akbar!" typically precedes thunderous bursts of machine gun fire and the detonations of bombs and missiles.

Extremist behavior, unfortunately, is nothing new to Islam. Although initially dubbed a "religion of peace," Islam ran into trouble just a couple of decades after Muhammad's death; in Islam's first twenty-nine years (from AD 632 to 661), three of the four initial caliphs were murdered. This violent trend continued with the political murders of Hassan and Husain, two sons of Ali, at the hands of their rival, Mayywia. Also, according to Shia doctrine, there are twelve main imams (preachers), starting with Ali, the first and rightful successor of Muhammad, and ending with Al-Mehdi. Out of these twelve, nine were poisoned and two were killed outright. (The last one, Al-Mehdi, supposedly survived and entered into a spiritually hidden state of being, where he still resides until he reappears with Jesus on Judgment Day.) This initial violence culminated in brutal crusades on the Iberian Peninsula in the eighth century. In the eleventh century, Islam invaded the Indian subcontinent, as well as other regions. In this context, it's hard to see Islam as a religion of peace. (Victims of the Spanish Inquisition would no doubt agree.) To add insult to injury, Islamic historical books, and many Muslims today, proudly acclaim the initial spread of Islam. They forget that most followers of other faiths find forced indoctrination repugnant; the victims of Islam had no choice but to convert at the time. Muslims carried the "sword of peace" in one hand and a Qur'an in the other, demanding that others "submit to the will of Allah." Christians of Spain, pagans of Persia, and Hindus of India lived in contentment with their gods—Jesus, Zoroaster, and the Bhagwan—for centuries until Islam arrived. They had never seen or heard of this new god, "Allah," before. Muslim raids were clearly an invasion of their territory and beliefs.

Today's victims of Islamic extremism (which also include progressive and moderate Muslims) still have their best chance of survival in the Western world. Many crushed and wounded activists who were expelled from their homelands for social, political, and religious reasons moved to London, not Mecca, to escape persecution. But many hard-core groups exploit certain guarantees of Western society, such as free speech and the right to congregate peacefully, and use them to their advantage. One radical Muslim group openly speculates about turning British cities into Islamic states; they would change the name of London to "Londonistan." The name of the group is Islamic Emirates, and their slogan is "End of Man-Made Law and Start of Sharia Law." Here are a few excerpts from their radical agenda to convert the world to Islam:

+ Muslims must follow Sharia Law and are not allowed to obey man-made laws.
+ Muslims must call for Sharia Law to be implemented wherever they are.
+ Any Muslim affected by the Western way of life needs to be rehabilitated.
+ Muslims must reject secularism and democracy.

It is worth noting here that Muslims aren't the only ones with radical extremist groups. There are many radical religions and social and cultural groups at work in the world, from neo-Nazis to antiabortion fundamentalist Christians. The agendas of these radicals represent unrealistic and far-fetched fantasies. In the case of Islam, promoters of the radical interpretation of Sharia Law would never have left their homelands of India, Pakistan, Bangladesh, and other Middle Eastern countries if Sharia Law worked properly. Britain's civil laws regarding health, housing, education, and social security cover all British nationals and residents, even newly arrived Muslims and non-Muslims. Radicals have no quarrels with Britain's civil laws as long as they can reap the benefits; they're like the starving man who received the chance to survive a year ago and now complains about his free meal of Kobe steak and Dom Perignon. If these young Muslim radicals in Britain were given a chance to visit their homelands for a week, they would go flying back to Britain at the first allowable instant. This would make great subject matter for a reality show called *Wake Up in Your Holy Land and Smell the Coffee!*

One of these "wake up and smell the coffee" moments would surely have to occur in Saudi Arabia. Accepted by many as the Islamic center of the world, Saudi Arabia ostensibly espouses a belief system of equality and fairness for all—or at least tolerance. Yet some of the worst discriminatory laws exist there. At various points in Mecca and Medina, public road signs are marked Exit—and these signs are exclusively for *nonbelievers*. The divine flag of Islam, the "religion of tolerance and peace," flies high above these exit signs. Imagine similar signs around the Vatican, marked Muslims Exit Here! How many lawsuits would that provoke? Saudi Arabian authorities, however, due to their warmth and generosity, allow non-Muslims to practice their religion in the privacy of their homes. Of course, many arrests occur in these in-house churches. Of note also is the fact that about 80 percent of US mosques are built and supported by funds from Saudi Arabia.[111]

---

[111] "Al Qaeda, Other Terror Groups Swim in Global Sea of Saudi-Funded Wahhabi Institutions," IslamicPluralism.org, last modified August 22, 2007, http://www.islamicpluralism.org/532/al-qaeda-other-terror-groups-swim-in-global-sea-of-saudi.

# 30

## In Conclusion: God Is Slowly Fading Away

At this point, we've seen how human beings created the notion of God out of their own needs and misunderstandings. Despite our ability to create tall buildings through logic and mathematics, we still go on creating God out of fear of dying and for all kinds of other reasons. God's humanlike thinking and behavior confirms that humans created God. We've examined the nature and character of God, and how His characteristics reflect humanity, with all its needs and wants. We've examined "miracles" and put them in their rightful place as natural or scientific phenomena. We've also examined many similarities that exist among the holy scriptures, suggesting that people simply borrowed and modified earlier texts to create their own "original" stories. We've considered the many troubling hypocrisies of God and His holy messengers and religious officials; it seems that behind their holy cloaks, they are all about getting and keeping power. Even more troubling is the wicked side of God—the God who kills and destroys at whim, and the humans who kill to acquire power in God's name.

Over the course of this book, we have also seen the importance of examining the concept of God in many contexts. If people are going to persist in creating notions of God, at least they should be aware of and take responsibility for *which* God they aid and abet. After considering all existing religious possibilities, people should be hard-pressed to think of a reason to believe in God, but there will always be some who do, at least for a while longer. The freedom to choose religion or faith must go hand in hand with an awareness of how these phenomena came into being and their impact on the world. Blind belief based on family tradition or because somebody said so just isn't a logical reason to espouse a religious view. Unless a person has thoroughly examined the historical roots of the concept of God and considered every major religious path, he or she is not in a position to take on the responsibility of choosing a faith—not when religion does more harm than good in the world. It is a serious matter to say that one is a Catholic, a Jew, a Muslim, a Hindu, or a Buddhist in today's world. Without any application of critical thinking to choosing religion, religion is better left alone.

In this day and age, it is inconceivable to think that seven American states assert in their constitutions that people who do not believe in God are not eligible to hold public office. These seven states are Maryland, Arkansas, Mississippi, North Carolina, South Carolina, Tennessee, and Texas. In terms of the total US population, this means that 19 percent, or sixty million Americans, may not become elected or appointed public servants based on that personal belief alone. This is a large number that represents a tremendous act of discrimination against nonbelievers (atheists). This discrimination stands without reason or logic—particularly in a country that proclaims equal opportunity for all. On the eve of his 1984 reelection, President Ronald Reagan extolled the virtues of American freedom, stating, "To a tired and disillusioned world, we have always been a new world and, yes, a shining city on a hill where all things are possible ... America that has a cause and a vision of future where all people can experience the warmth and hope of individual liberty."[112] Apparently, as so many politicians do today, President Reagan conveniently ignored rampant discrimination toward nonbelievers. How can our society deny the possibility of holding public office to so many based solely on their personal or religious beliefs? Shouldn't holding public office be based on one's sincerity and abilities? Other minorities,

---

[112] Presidency.UCSB.edu, http://www.presidency.ucsb.edu/ws/index.php?pid= 39385&st=city+on+a+hill&st1=
President Ronald Reagan, Address to the nation on eve of Presidential election 1984. November 5, 1984.

such as gays and lesbians, have slowly moved to the front of the bus—that is, to a more accepted status in society—but one has to wonder if nonbelievers will ever get there.

The good news is that technology, something based on logic and fact, has already started to reform a significant portion of the human race. Today, 2.01 percent of the world's population is atheist, while 16 percent is nonreligious.[113] At this rate, the next five hundred years should see religious fanatics become the minority. Belief in an invisible God is slowly fading away. In biblical times, God came to the select few and left them to carry out His will with the words "The Lord said so." God then passed the baton to His handpicked holy messengers. Now the messages are worn out, the baton lies broken, and God's repeated messages have become old and useless, as they have not produced any fruitful results. Despite God's efforts, humanity has not changed its errant ways. God enviously saw the dawn of the twenty-first-century generation—Coke in one hand, computer in the other—performing more interesting and useful "miracles." These miracles are better, faster, and more efficient than Moses throwing his rod, Jesus walking on water, or Muhammad traveling to heaven on a winged horse. They are also visible, palpable, and provable. Some people will go on choosing concept over logic and fact, and in the name of blind faith, they will overlook God's many faux pas. But those who seriously undertake the journey of choosing a religion will undoubtedly find that the more they dig into holy scriptures, the more God fades away in the rearview mirror.

---

[113] "Demographics of Atheism," *Wikipedia*, last modified October 9, 2014, http://en.wikipedia.org/wiki/Demographics_of_atheism.

# ACKNOWLEDGMENT

I would like to express my sincere gratitude to Kathira Nemand for her many sincere thoughts and contribution throughout the editing sequence.

Kathira, thank you for your skills, expertise, and genuine views in editing. It was a great pleasure working with you.

# Index

## A

Aaron, 52, 117, 133
Abel, 50, 82, 83, 104
Abigail, 105
Abimelech (king), 89
Abishag, 105
Abraham
    belief in one God, 29–30
    circumcision and, 53, 88
    as friend of God, 14
    Hajj and, 140
    as holy messenger, 3, 30
    justifies actions, 84–90
    Lot and, 133
    Muhammad and, 161–162
    numbers and, 159–160
    proof and, 181
    sacrifice and, 135–137
Abu-Bakr, 6, 133, 155–157
Adam, 9, 42, 47, 49–50, 67, 81, 83,
    109–110, 178
Afghanistan, 149, 150
afterlife, 20–21, 24, 33, 61, 92, 174, 180
Agag, 107–108
Agricultural Revolution, 39

Ai, 54
Aisha, 156, 157, 166
Akbar the Great, 115
Ali, Yusuf, 62, 65, 67, 82, 101, 148, 151,
    153, 154–155, 156, 158–159
Ali Baba and the Forty Thieves, 179
Ali bin Abu Talib, 155–157
Allah, 2, 5, 28, 30, 31, 32, 40, 57, 74,
    143, 162
Allegory of the Cave, 124
Amenphis IV (King), 37
angels, 3, 75–77, 88, 109, 115–116, 178
Anselm, St., 129
apostles, 51, 70, 83–84
Aquinas, St. Thomas, 126–129
Arabic language, 153
Arafat, Yasser, 100
architecture, 181–182
Arda Viraf, 151, 163
Aristotle, 151
Arjuna, 175–176
atheism, 189–190
atoms, 151–153
Aton, 37

Atum, 28, 29, 31
Augustine, St., 129

Aung San Suu Kyi, 101

# B

# C

# D

# E

# F

# G

natural disasters and, 67–68

obedience and, 25–26

Old Testament *vs.* New Testament, 1, 23

omniscience of, 7, 50–51, 83–84, 109–110

perfection of, 9, 113, 128

power and, 2–3, 111

promises of, 53

proofs of, 126–129

punishment and, 11, 15, 23–24, 26

Satan and, 9, 109–110, 177–178

sense of mystery and, 46

veiled messages of, 78–79

Goebbels, Joseph, 16

good and evil, 177

Gospels, 6, 79–80

*See also names of individual books*

Great Britain, 115

great flood, 18–19, 108, 160–161, 162

Greek mythology, 15, 19

Gregory VII (pope), 36–37

grief, 20–21

# H

Hadiths, 80–81, 113, 138, 165

Hafsa, 156, 157

Hagar, 77, 86, 140, 159–160, 161

Hajj, 30, 139–141

Hammurabi, Code of, 94, 101–102, 151

Haran, 89, 90

hearts, 22

heliocentric theory, 133–134

hell, 9

Henry IV (Emperor), 36–37

Henry VIII (king), 1, 98

Hercules, 99, 164–165

high priests, 35–36

hijab, 149–150

Hindu Milk Miracle, 43

Hindu mythology, 19–20

Hinduism, 131, 139–141, 163

Hitler Youth, 169

Holy Bible. *See* Bible

holy messengers

angels as, 75

bending the rules, 96–98

contradictions and, 149

God's need for, 7

mythical stories about, 163–166

number of, 159

personal agendas of, 13

proof and, 5–6

religious populations and, 73–74

sidekicks of, 133

as smooth talkers, 92

threats and, 25

twisted meanings, 90

veiled messages and, 79

Holy Qur'an. *See* Qur'an

Holy Trinity. *See* Trinity

holy wars, 63–64

human sacrifice, 135–137

Hurricane Katrina, 68, 108

hygiene, 65–66

# I

Ibn-Hanbal, 159

Ibn-Muja-Hid, 155

incest, 104

India, 66, 139–141

Iran, 143

Iraq, 81

Isaac, 85, 89, 136, 137, 160

Isaf, 30

Ishmael, 77, 86, 136, 140, 159–160, 161

Isis, 32

Islam
    Allah, 31, 32
    black stone of Mecca, 4–5, 29–30
    bowing to God's will, 72–74,
        148, 162
    caliphs and, 157
    extremists and, 183–187
    Hajj and, 30, 139–141
    hijab and, 149–150
    hygiene and, 65–66
    idol worship and, 4–5, 29
    Jews and, 162
    marriage and, 40
    moon and, 5
    not first religion, 83
    prayer method of, 30
    religious populations and, 74
    sects of, 81
    seventh heaven, 6
    Sufism, 35
    violent history of, 185
    women and, 149–150
    *See also* Muhammad

Islamic Emirates, 186

Israelites, 52–54, 57

# J

Jacob, 31, 37, 86, 117

Jephthah, 136, 137

Jesus
    birth stories, 66–67, 75–76
    God's abandonment, 13, 53
    Gospel stories of, 79–80
    heavenly rewards and, 24
    as holy messenger, 3
    John the Baptist and, 133
    as part of God, 10
    Sabbath and, 119
    table of food for, 117

John, 6, 10

John Paul II (pope), 134, 169, 172

John the Baptist, 6, 133

Joshua, 53–54, 134

Jubilees, Book of, 88

Judah, 55

Judaism, 3, 81, 83, 151

Judge Samuel, 107–108

justice, 102–103

# K

Kanada, 151, 152

Keturah, 161

Khadija, 133

Khadir, 156

Khaybar, 96

Khomeini, Ayatollah, 143, 184

Kings, Books of, 105, 106, 135

Krishna, 5, 140–141, 174–176

Kulthum, 157

Kumbh Mela, 139–141

# L

Lakshmi, 163

leadership, 95, 100–101

Leah, 86

Leo IX (pope), 36

Leviticus, 23, 26, 91
Lord Krishna. *See* Krishna
Lord Vishnu. *See* Vishnu

luck, 117–118, 120
Luke, 6, 67, 79

# M

Magus, Simon, 168
Makkedah, 54
Mandela, Nelson, 101, 124
Mark, 6, 79, 80
marriage, 39–41
Mary. *See* Virgin Mary
*Masqala Zarrah*, 151–153
Matthew, 6, 24, 63, 67, 79
Mecca, 4–5, 29–30, 87, 119, 139–141,
    161, 187
miracles, 42–46, 119–120
Miraj, 137–138, 163, 165–166
money, 56
monotheism, 1, 4, 15–16, 31, 37, 66, 81
moon, 5
Moses
    Aaron and, 133
    communication with God, 86,
        117–118
    God's involvement with
    humans, 58–59
    good old days and, 8–9
    as holy messenger, 3, 124
    infancy of, 18–19

justifies actions, 90–92
Mount Nebo, 52–53
on Mount Sinai, 12–13, 14
Muhammad and, 162
names of God, 31
signs for, 116–117
Superman and, 45–46
Ten Commandments and, 93–94
throwing rod, 119–120
Motion, Theory of, 126–127
Mount Sinai, 12–13, 14
Muhammad
    Abraham and, 161–162
    dictation of Qur'an, 153, 155, 159
    Hadiths and, 80–81
    as holy messenger, 3
    justifies behavior, 96–97
    marriages of, 157
    Night Journey of, 113, 137–138,
        163, 165–166
    sidekicks and, 133
    starts Islam, 74, 148
    *See also* Islam
Muslims. *See* Islam

# N

Nabal, 105
Nailai, 30
names, importance of, 32
Nazis, 16
Nebertcher, 18
New Testament, 1, 151
Nicene Creed, 130

Night Journey, 113, 137–138, 163,
    165–166
Nimrod, 131
Nirvana, 145–146
Noah, 3, 18, 24–25, 26, 108, 160–161
Norse gods, 14, 15, 18, 27
Numbers, Book of, 44

# O

# P

# Q

Printed in the United States
By Bookmasters